The
LITTLE BLACK
SONGBOOK

ITS

ISBN: 978-1-84772-986-6

Visit Hal Leonard Online at
www.halleonard.com

World headquarters,contact:
Hal Leonard
7777 West Bluemound Road
Milwaukee, WI 53213
Email: info@halleonard.com

In Europe, contact:
Hal Leonard Europe Limited
1 Red Place
London, W1K 6PL
Email: info@halleonardeurope.com

In Australia, contact:
Hal Leonard Australia Pty. Ltd.
4 Lentara Court
Cheltenham, Victoria, 3192 Australia
Email: info@halleonard.com.au

Relative Tuning

The guitar can be tuned with the aid of pitch pipes or dedicated electronic guitar tuners which are available through your local music dealer. If you do not have a tuning device, you can use relative tuning. Estimate the pitch of the 6th string as near as possible to E or at least a comfortable pitch (not too high, as you might break other strings in tuning up). Then, while checking the various positions on the diagram, place a finger from your left hand on the:

5th fret of the E or 6th string and **tune the open A** (or 5th string) to the note Ⓐ

5th fret of the A or 5th string and **tune the open D** (or 4th string) to the note Ⓓ

5th fret of the D or 4th string and **tune the open G** (or 3rd string) to the note Ⓖ

4th fret of the G or 3rd string and **tune the open B** (or 2nd string) to the note Ⓑ

5th fret of the B or 2nd string and **tune the open E** (or 1st string) to the note Ⓔ

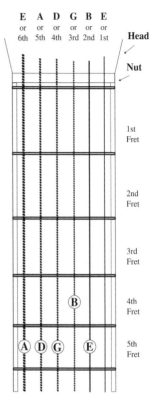

Reading Chord Boxes

Chord boxes are diagrams of the guitar neck viewed head upwards, face on as illustrated. The top horizontal line is the nut, unless a higher fret number is indicated, the others are the frets.

The vertical lines are the strings, starting from E (or 6th) on the left to E (or 1st) on the right.

The black dots indicate where to place your fingers.

Strings marked with an O are played open, not fretted. Strings marked with an X should not be played.

The curved bracket indicates a 'barre' - hold down the strings under the bracket with your first finger, using your other fingers to fret the remaining notes.

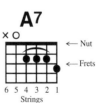

Alice

Words & Music by Tom Waits & Kathleen Brennan

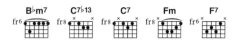

Verse 1

              B♭m7   **C7♭13** **C7**
It's dreamy weather we're on,

              Fm   **F7**
You wave your crooked wand,

           B♭m7   **C7♭13** **C7**
Along an icy pond with a frozen moon.

         Fm   **B♭m7**
A murder of silhouette crows I saw,

            C7♭13 **C7**
And the tears on my face,

            B♭m7 **C7**   **Fm**
And the skates on the pond,   they spell Alice.

Verse 2

B♭m7   **C7♭13** **C7**
   I'll disappear in your name,

         Fm   **F7**
But you must wait for me.

         B♭m7
Somewhere a - cross the sea,

            C7♭13 **C7**
There's the wreck of a ship.

          F7   **B♭m7**
Your hair is like meadow grass on the tide.

          C7♭13   **C7**
And the raindrops on my window,

        B♭m7 **C7**
And the ice in my drink,

          B♭m7 **C7** **Fm**
Baby, all that I can think of   is Alice.

Verse 3

B♭m7   C7♭13   C7
   Arithmetic, a - rithmetock,

Fm   F7
   I turn the hands back on the clock.

B♭m7   C7
   How does the ocean   rock the boat,

Fm   F7
How did the razor find my throat?

B♭m7   C7♭13   C7
   The only strings that hold me here,

   B♭m7   C7
Are tangled up around the pier.

Verse 4

         B♭m7   C7♭13 C7
And so a secret kiss,

            Fm   F7
Brings madness with the bliss.

       B♭m7
And I will think of this,

       C7♭13   C7
When I'm dead in my grave.

      Fm   B♭m7
Set me adrift   and I'm lost   over there.

      C7♭13 C7
And I must be in - sane,

         B♭m7 C7
To go skating on your name,

       B♭m7   C7
And by tracing it twice,

    B♭m7   C7 Fm
I fell through the ice of Alice.

Sax. solo

| B♭m7 C7♭13 C7 | Fm   F7 | B♭m7 | |

| C7♭13 C7 | Fm B♭m7 | B♭m7 C7 |

Verse 5

       B♭m7   **C7♭13** **C7**
And so a secret kiss,

           Fm   **F7**
Brings madness with the bliss.

B♭m7
  And I will think of this,

           C7♭13   **C7**
When I'm dead in my grave.

   Fm   **B♭m7**
Set me   adrift and I'm lost   over there.

          C7♭13 **C7**
And I must be in - sane,

              B♭m7 **C7**
To go skating on your name,

            B♭m7   **C7**
And by tracing it twice,

     B♭m7   **C7**   **Fm**
I fell through the ice   of Alice.

    C7♭13 **C7**   **Fm**
There's only   A - lice.

All The World Is Green

Words & Music by Tom Waits & Kathleen Brennan

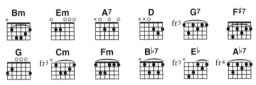

Intro   ‖: Bm | Bm :‖ *Play 3 times*

Verse 1

       Bm   Em
    I fell into the ocean,

      A7   D
    When you became my wife.

    G7   F♯7
    I risked it all against the sea,

             Bm
To have a better life.

          Em   A7
Marie you are the wild blue sky,

             D
And men do fool - ish things.

G7   F♯7
   You turn kings into beggars,

            Bm
And beggars into kings.

Chorus 1

          G   D
Pre - tend that you owe me nothing,

       A7   D
And all the world is green.

G   D
   We can bring back the old days again,

       A7   D
When all the world is green.

Verse 2

    Bm   **Em**
    The face forgives   the mirror,

A⁷   **D**
    The worm forgives the plow.

G⁷   **F♯7**
    The questions begs the answer;

              Bm
Can you forgive me somehow?

          Em   **A⁷**
Maybe when our story's over,

              D
We'll go where it's al - ways spring.

G⁷   **F♯7**
    The band is play - ing our song again,

              Bm
And all the world is green.

Chorus 2

     G   **D**
Pre - tend that you owe me nothing,

    A⁷   **D**
And all the world is green.

G   **D**
    Can we bring back the old days again,

    A⁷   **D**
When all the world is green?

Verse 3

Bm   **Em**
    The moon is yel - low silver,

A⁷   **D**
    On the things that summer brings.

G⁷   **F♯7**
    It's a love you'd kill for,

              Bm
And all the world is green.

          Em   **A⁷**
He's balancing   a diamond,

          D
On a blade of grass.

G⁷   **F♯7**
    The dew will settle on our graves,

            Bm
When all the world is green.

Chorus 3
        G   D
Pre - tend that you owe me nothing,

     A7   D
And all the world is green.

G   D
  We can bring back the old days again,

     A7   D   G7
When all the world is green.

Instrumental ‖: Cm | Fm | B♭7 | E♭ |

               | A♭7 | G7 | G7 | Cm :‖

Verse 4
Cm   Fm
  He's balanc - ing a diamond,

B♭7   E♭
On a blade of grass.

A♭7   G7
  The dew will set - tle on our graves,

            Cm
When all the world is green.

Outro ‖: Cm | Cm | Cm | Cm :‖

Anywhere I Lay My Head

Words & Music by Tom Waits

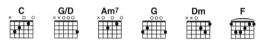

C   G/D   Am⁷   G   Dm   F

Capo first fret

Verse 1

    C   G/D   C
My head is spinning round,

       Am⁷   G
My heart is in my shoes, yeah.

Dm   G
I went and set the Thames on fire,

                        C
Now I must come back down.

F   C
She's laughing in her sleeve boys,

F   Dm   G
I can feel it in my bones.

          C   G/D
Oh, but anywhere, anywhere,

      C   F
I'm gonna lay my head,

         C   G/D C G
Oh, I'm gonna call my home.___

Verse 2

```
        C                      G/D          C
        Well I see that the world is up - side down, yeah,
                               Am7                   G
        Seems that my pockets were filled up with gold.
        Dm                                            G
          And now the clouds, well, they've covered everything over,
                              C
        And the wind is blowing cold.
        F                    C
          Well, I don't need any - body,
                    F                    Dm   G
        Because I learned, I learned to be a - lone.
                    C        G/D
        But I said anywhere, anywhere,
                 C                F
        Any - where I lay my head, boys,
        C          G/D    C
        Well I gotta call my home.
```

Outro

```
‖: C  G/D │ C      │ C      │ G      │

   │ Dm     │ G      │ G      │ C      │

   │ F      │ C      │ F      │ Dm  G  │

   │ C  G/D │ C  F   │ C  G/D │ C  G  :‖   Repeat to fade
```

15

Big In Japan

Words & Music by Tom Waits & Kathleen Brennan

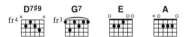

Intro | D7♯9 | D7♯9 | D7♯9 | D7♯9 ‖

Verse 1

D7♯9
I got the style but not the grace.

I got the clothes but not the face.

I got the bread but not the butter.

I got the window but not the shutter.

Chorus 1

D7♯9
But I'm big in Japan,

I'm big in Japan,

Hey, but I'm big in Japan,

I'm big in Japan.

Verse 2

D7♯9
I got the house but not the deed.

I got the horn but not the reed.

I got the cards but not the luck.

I got the wheel but not the truck.

Chorus 2

D7♯9
But hey I'm big in Japan,

I'm big in Japan,

But hey, I'm big in Japan,

I'm big in Japan.

Bridge 1

       G7   **D7♯9**
I got the moon, I got the cheese,
       G7   **D7♯9**
I got the whole damn nation on their knees.
       G7   **D7♯9**
I got the rooster, I got the crow,
       E   **A**
I got the ebb, I got the flow.

Verse 3

D7♯9
I got the powder but not the gun.

I got the dog but not the bun.

I got the clouds but not the sky.

I got the stripes but not the tie.

Chorus 3

D7♯9
But hey I'm big in Japan,

I'm big in Japan,

I'm big in Japan,

I'm big in Japan,

I'm big in Japan.

Guitar solo   ‖: **D7♯9** | **D7♯9** | **D7♯9** | **D7♯9** :‖

Link 1

N.C.
Hey ho, they love the way I do it.

Hey ho, there's really nothing to it.

Bridge 2   As Bridge 1

Verse 4

D7♯9
I got the sizzle but not the steak.

I got the boat but not the lake.

I got the sheets but not the bed.

I got the jam but not the bread.

Chorus 4

D7♯9
But hey I'm big in Japan,

I'm big in Japan,

I'm big in Japan,

I'm big in Japan.

| **D7♯9** | **D7♯9** | **D7♯9** | |

D7♯9
I'm big in Japan,

I'm big in Japan.

Outro   ‖: **D7♯9** | **D7♯9** | **D7♯9** | **D7♯9** :‖

18

Black Wings

Words & Music by Tom Waits & Kathleen Brennan

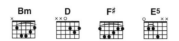

Intro | Bm | Bm | Bm | Bm ‖

Verse 1
Bm
Well, take an eye for an eye,

A tooth for a tooth,
        D   **F♯**
Just like they say in the Bible,
        Bm
But never leave a trace or forget a face,
        D   **F♯**
Of any man at the table,
                        Bm
Any man at the ta - ble.

Chorus 1
(**Bm**)   **E5**   **Bm**
When the moon is a cold chiseled dagger,
        E5   **Bm**
And it's sharp enough to draw blood from a stone,
E5   **Bm**
    He rides through your dreams on a coach and horses,
        E5   **F♯**
And the fence posts in the moonlight look like bones.

Verse 2

(F#)   **Bm**

Well, they've stopped trying to hold him,

With mortar, stone and chain,

D   **F#**

  He broke out of every prison.

        Bm

Well, the boots mount the staircase,

The door is flung back open,

D   **F#**

He's not there for he has risen,

          Bm

He's not there for he has risen.

Chorus 2

E5   **Bm**

Some say he once killed a man with a gui - tar string,

  E5   **Bm**

He's been seen at the table with kings.

    E5   **Bm**

Well, he once saved a baby from drowning,

     E5   **F#**

There are those that say beneath his coat there are wings.

     Bm   **D** **F#**

Well, some say they fear him.

Instrumental

| Bm | Bm | Bm | Bm | |
| D | F# | F# | F# | ‖ |

‖: Bm | Bm | E5 | E5 :‖ *Play 4 times*

| F# | F# | ‖ |

Verse 3

Bm

  Well, some say they fear him,

Others admire him,

   D   **F#**

Be - cause he steals his promise.

cont.

Bm
One look in his eye,

And everyone denies,

D   **F♯**
Ever having met him,

Bm
Ever having met him.

Chorus 3

E5   **Bm**
He can turn himself into a stranger,

E5   **Bm**
Well, they broke a lot of canes on his hide.

E5   **Bm**
He was born away in a cornfield,

E5   **F♯**
A fever beats in his head just like a drum inside.

Verse 4

Bm
Some say they fear him,

Others admire him,

D   **F♯**
Because he steals his promise.

Bm
One look in his eye,

Everyone denies,

F♯   **Bm**
Ever having met him,

F♯   **Bm**
Ever having met him,

F♯   **Bm**
Ever having met him,

F♯   **Bm**
Ever having met him,

F♯   **Bm**
Ever having met him,

F♯   **Bm**
Ever having met him.

Outro   **‖: F♯** | **Bm** | **F♯** | **Bm** :‖

Blind Love

Words & Music by Tom Waits

Capo first fret

Intro | A | D | A | A   ‖

Verse 1

(A)
Now you're gone,

     D   **A**
It's   hotels and whiskey   and sad-luck dames,

And I don't care if they miss me,

D   **G**   **E**
   I never remember their names.

                 A   **D**
They say if you get far enough away,

          A   **D**
You'll be on your way back home,

          A   **D**   **G**   **E**
Well, I'm at the station and I can't get on the train.

Chorus 1

(E)   **D**   **A**
Must be blind love, only kind of love is stone blind love.

E   **A/C♯** **D**   **A7**
Blind love, only kind of love is stone blind love.

          D   **A**   **E**
With your blind love, oh it's blind love, stone blind love,

             D   **A**
It's your stone blind love.

Verse 2

A
Now the street's turning blue,

      D   A
The dogs are barking and the night has come,

                         D   G   E
There's tears that are falling   from your blue eyes now.

    A   D A   D
And I wonder where you are   and I whisper your name,

A   D   G   E
The only way to find you is if I close my eyes.

Chorus 2

(E)   D
I'll find you with my blind love,

                      A
The only kind of love is stone blind love.

                     E
The only kind of love is stone blind love.

                    A/C# D   A7
The only kind of love is stone blind love.

            D   A
With your blind love, oh your blind love,

E   D   A
   Your stone blind love.

Instrumental

‖: A | D | A | A |

| A | D | G | E   :‖

Chorus 3

(E)   D
It's your blind love,

                      A
The only kind of love is stone blind love.

E
Stone blind love,

                  A/C# D   A7
The only kind of love is stone blind love.

            D
With your blind love,

                    A
The only kind of love is   stone blind love.

E   D   A
Stone blind love, stone blind love.

The Briar And The Rose

Words & Music by Tom Waits

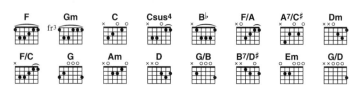

Verse 1

```
     F        Gm   C      F
     I fell a - sleep down by the stream,
            Gm     Csus4 C      F
And there I   had the    strang - est dream.
B♭          F/A              A7/G♯    Dm
   And down by Brennan's      Glenn there grows,
Gm      C       F
   A briar   and a rose.
Dm                  C
   There's a tree in the forest,
B♭          F/A
   But I don't know where.
B♭          F/A      Gm        C
   And I built a nest out   of your hair.
F               C  F      B♭
   And climbing up into the    air,
F/C     C       F
   A briar and a rose.
```

Verse 2

```
     G    Am          D    G
     I don't know how long   it has been,
            Am  D           G
But I was born   in Brennan's Glenn.
C              G/B   B7/F♯    Em
   And near the    end of spring there grows
Am       D       G
   A briar   and a rose.
```

cont.

```
Em          D    C      G/B
I picked the rose one ear - ly morn',
C         G           Am  D
  I pricked my finger on a thorn.
G           D        G           C
  It'd grown so close, the winding wove,
G/D            D          G
  The briar a - round the rose.
```

Verse 3

```
G      Am        D        G
  I tried to tear them   both a - part,
      Am    D      G
I felt a bullet   in my heart.
C        G/B        B7/D#      Em
  And all dressed up in spring's new clothes,
Am          D      G
  The bri - ar and the rose.
Em          D       C   G/B
  And when I'm bu - ried in my grave,
C      G      Am      D
  Tell me so I will know.
G          D        G         C
Your tears will fall   to make love grow,
G/D            D       G
  The briar and the rose.
```

Outro

```
Em          D       C   G/B
  And when I'm bu - ried in my grave,
C      G      Am      D
  Tell me so I will know.
      G         D  G        C
Your tears will fall to make them grow,
G/D            D      G
  The briar and the rose.
      G         D  G        C
Your tears will fall to make them grow,
      G/D  D      G
The briar and the   rose.
```

Blue Valentines

Words & Music by Tom Waits

Intro | Dm9 | E9 | Dm9 | E9 | Dm9 | E9 |

Verse 1

                           Dm7 E9
She sends me, blue valentines,

           Dm7   **E9**
All the way from Phila - delphia.

          Dm7   **E9**
To mark the anni - versary,

          Am7   **A7**
Of someone that I used to be.

          Dm7   **E9**
And it feels like a warrant,

Am7   **A7**
Out for my ar - rest.

                     Dm7   **E9**   **Am7**   **A7**
Baby, you got me checking in my rearview mirror,

              Dm7   **E9**
That's why I'm always on the run.

          Am7
That's why I changed my name,

     B7   **E9**
And I didn't think you'd ever find me here.

Verse 2

Dm7 E9
To send me, blue   valentines,

Dm7   E9
Like half-forgotten dreams.

Dm7   E9
Like a pebble in my shoe,

Am7   A7
As I walk these streets.

Dm7   E9
And the ghost of your memory,

Am7   A7
Baby, is the thistle in the kiss.

Dm7   E9   Am7 A7
It's the burgler that can break a rose's neck.

Dm7   E9   Am7
It's the tattooed broken promise I got to hide beneath my sleeve,

B7   E9
I'm gonna see you every time I turn my back.

Solo

| Dm7 E9 | Dm7 E9 | Dm7 E9 | Am7 A7 |

| Dm7 E9 | Am7 A7 | Dm7 E9 | Am7 A7 |

| Dm7 E9 | Am7 | B7 | E9 ‖

Verse 3

        Dm7 **E9**
She sends me blue valentines,

    Dm7   **E9**
Though I try to re - main at large.

      Dm7   **E9**
They're in - sisting that our love,

      Am7   **A7**
Must have a eulogy.

      Dm7   **E9**
Why do I save all this madness,

       Am7   **A7**
Here in the nightstand drawer.

     Dm7   **E9**
There to haunt upon my shoulders,

     Am7 **A7**
Baby I know.

     Dm7   **E9**   **Am7**
I'd be luckier to walk around everywhere I go,

     B7
With a blind and broken heart,

        E9
That sleeps be - neath my lapel.

Verse 4

      Dm7 **E9**
Instead, these blue valentines,

  Dm7   **E9**
To remind me of my cardinal sin.

    Dm7   **E9**
I can never wash the guilt,

        Am7   **A7**
Or get these bloodstains off my hands.

     Dm7   **E9**
And it takes a whole lot of whiskey,

  Am7   **A7**
To make this nightmares go away.

     Dm7   **E9**   **Am7** **A7**
And I cut my bleeding heart out every night.

          Dm7   **E9**   **Am7**
And I'm gonna die just a little more on each St. Valentine's day.

    B7   **E9**
Don't you remember I promised I would write you,

     Dm7 **E9**
These blue valentines,

Dm9 **E9**   **Dm9** **E9**   **Am9**
Blue valentines, blue valen - tines.

Burma Shave

Words & Music by Tom Waits

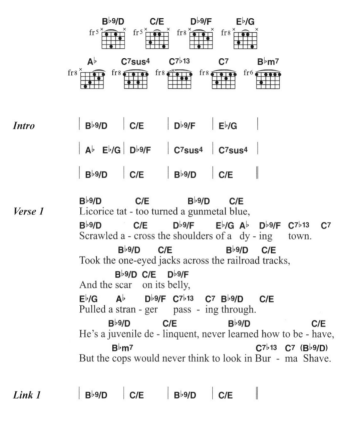

Intro
| B♭9/D | C/E | D♭9/F | E♭/G |
| A♭ E♭/G D♭9/F | C7sus4 | C7sus4 |
| B♭9/D | C/E | B♭9/D | C/E ‖

Verse 1

B♭9/D   C/E   B♭9/D   C/E
Licorice tat - too turned a gunmetal blue,

B♭9/D   C/E   D♭9/F   E♭/G A♭   D♭9/F   C7♭13   C7
Scrawled a - cross the shoulders of a   dy - ing   town.

        B♭9/D   C/E   B♭9/D   C/E
Took the one-eyed jacks across the railroad tracks,

          B♭9/D C/E   D♭9/F
And the scar   on its belly,

E♭/G   A♭   D♭9/F C7♭13   C7 B♭9/D   C/E
Pulled a stran - ger   pass - ing through.

         B♭9/D   C/E   B♭9/D   C/E
He's a juvenile de - linquent, never learned how to be - have,

       B♭m7   C7♭13   C7   (B♭9/D)
But the cops would never think to look in Bur - ma Shave.

Link 1
| B♭9/D | C/E | B♭9/D | C/E ‖

Verse 2

     B♭m7   C7♭13   B♭9/D   C/E
And the road was like a ribbon and the moon was like a bone,

  B♭9/D C/E   D♭9/F E♭/G A♭   D♭9/F C7♭13   C7
He didn't seem to be like any guy she'd ever   known.

      B♭9/D   C/E   B♭9/D   C/E
He kinda looked like Farley Granger with his hair slicked back,

         B♭9/D C/E D♭9/F E♭/G A♭   D♭9/F C7♭13   C7
She says "I'm a sucker for a fella in a cow - boy   hat.

   B♭9/D   C/E   B♭9/D   C/E
How far are you going?" he said "De - pends on what you mean."

       B♭m7   C7♭13
He says "I'm only stopping here to get some gaso - line.

  B♭9/D   C/E   B♭9/D   C/E
I guess I'm going that-a-way just as long as it's paved,

    B♭m7   C7♭13 (B♭9/D)
And I guess you'd say I'm on my way to Burma Shave."

Link 2 | B♭9/D | C/E | B♭9/D | C/E   ‖

            B♭m7   C7♭13
Verse 3   And with her knees up on the glove com - partment,

       B♭9/D   C/E   B♭9/D   C/E   D♭9/F   E♭/G
She took out her bar - rettes and her hair spilled out like rootbeer.

        A♭   D♭9/F   C7♭13   C7
And she popped her gum and arched her back,

      B♭9/D   C/E   B♭9/D   C/E
"Hell, Marysville ain't nothing but a wide spot in the road.

       B♭m7
Some nights my heart pounds like thunder,

      C7♭13   C7
Don't know why it don't ex - plode.

        B♭9/D   C/E   B♭9/D   C/E
'Cause everyone in this stinking town has got one foot in the grave,

    B♭m7   C7♭13 (B♭9/D)
And I'd rather take my chances out in Burma Shave."

Link 3 | B♭9/D | C/E | B♭9/D | C/E   ‖

     B♭9/D   C/E   B♭9/D   C/E
Verse 4   "Presley's what I go by, why   don't you change the station?

           B♭9/D C/E   D♭9/F E♭/G A♭   D♭9/F C7♭13   C7
Count the grain e - le - vators in the rear - view mirror."

                  B♭9/D   **C/E**
She said, "Mister, anywhere you point this thing,
         B♭9/D   **C/E**
Has got to beat the hell out of the sting,
     B♭9/D **D♭9/F** **C7♭13** **C7**   **B♭9/D**   **C/E**
Of going to bed with every dream that dies here every morning.
         B♭m7   **C7♭13**   **B♭9/D**   **C/E**
And so drill me a hole with a barber pole,
         B♭m7   **C7♭13 C7**   **B♭9/D**   **C/E**
And I'm jumping my pa - role   just like a fugitive to - night.
          B♭m7   **C7♭13 C7**
Why don't you   have another swig,
          B♭9/D   **C/E**
And pass that car if you're so brave,
         B♭m7   **C7♭13** **C7** **(B♭9/D)**
I wanna get there before the sun comes up in Bur - ma Shave."

Link 4 | **B♭9/D** | **C/E** | **B♭9/D** | **C/E**   ‖

         B♭9/D **C/E** **D♭9/F** **E♭/G**   **A♭**   **D♭9/F** **C7♭13** **C7**
Verse 5   And the spider web crack and the mus - tang   screamed,
    B♭9/D **C/E**   **D♭9/F** **E♭/G**   **A♭**   **D♭9/F** **C7♭13** **C7**
Smoke from the tires   and the twist - ed ma - chine.
       B♭9/D   **C/E**   **B♭9/D**   **C/E**
Just a nickel's worth of dreams and every wishbone that they saved,
       B♭m7   **C7♭13** **(B♭9/D)**
Lie swindled from them on the way to Burma Shave.

Link 5 | **B♭9/D** | **C/E** | **B♭9/D** | **C/E**   ‖

           B♭m7   **C7♭13** **C7**   **B♭9/D**   **C/E**
Verse 6   And the sun hit the der - rick and cast a bat-wing shadow,
  B♭m7   **C7♭13** **C7**   **B♭9/D**   **C/E**
Up against the car   door on the shotgun side.
            B♭m7   **C7♭13** **C7**
And when they   pulled her from the wreck,
          B♭9/D   **C/E**
You know she still had on her shades.
          B♭m7
They say that dreams are growing wild,
            C7♭13 **C7** **(B♭9/D)**
Just this side of Bur - ma Shave.

Outro | **B♭9/D** | **C/E** | **B♭9/D** | **C/E** | **B♭9/D**   ‖

Chocolate Jesus

Words & Music by Tom Waits & Kathleen Brennan

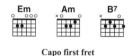

Capo first fret

Intro

| Em | Em | Em | Am | |
| Am | Em | B7 | Em ‖

Verse 1

      Em
Well, I don't go to church on Sunday,
              Am
Don't get on my knees to pray,
                    Em
Don't memorize the books of the Bible,
B7
I got my own special way.
Em
I know Jesus loves me,
           Am
Maybe just a little bit more,
                Em
I fall down on my knees every Sunday,
      B7   **Em**
At Ze - relda Lee's candy store.

Chorus 1

        Em
Well it's got to be a chocolate Jesus,
             Am
Make me feel good in - side.
          Em
Got to be a chocolate Jesus,
B7   **Em**
Keep me satis - fied.

Verse 2

      Em
Well I don't want no Abba Zabba,

            Am
Don't want no Almond Joy.

       Em
There ain't nothing better,

   B7
That's suitable for this boy.

       Em
Well, it's the only thing that can pick me up,

It's better than a cup of gold.

         Em
See only a chocolate Jesus,

  B7   **Em**
Can satisfy my soul.

Harmonica solo

Em	Em	Em	Am	
Am	Em	B7	B7	
Em	Em	Em	Am	
Am	Em	B7	Em	

Bridge

    Am
When the weather gets rough,

And it's whiskey in the shade,

          Em
It's best to wrap your saviour up in cellophane.

  Am
He flows like the big muddy, but that's OK,

B7
Pour him over ice cream for a nice parfait.

Chorus 2

     Em
Well, it's got to be a chocolate Jesus,

       Am
Good enough for me.

       Em
Got to be a chocolate Jesus,

  B7   **Em**
It's good enough for me.

Chorus 3

                  Em
Well it's got to be a chocolate Jesus,

                        Am
Make me feel so good in - side.

                   Em
Got to be a chocolate Jesus,

B7   **Em**
Keep me satis - fied.

Outro

Em	Em	Em	Am
Am	Em	B7	Em
B7	Em	B7	Em

Cold Cold Ground

Words & Music by Tom Waits

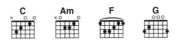

Intro ‖: C | Am | C | Am :‖ *Play 3 times*

Verse 1
    C   Am
Crestfallen sidekick in an old cafe,
          C   Am
Never slept with a dream before he had to go away.
        C   Am
There's a bell in the tower Uncle Ray bought a round,
      F   G   C
Don't worry about the army in the cold, cold ground.

       Am
Cold, cold ground,
       C
Cold, cold ground,
       Am
Cold, cold ground.

Verse 2
              C   Am
Now don't be a cry baby when there's wood in the shed,
       C   Am
There's a bird in the chimney and a stone in my bed.
         C   Am
When the road's washed out they pass the bottle around,
      F   G   C
And wait in the arms of the cold, cold ground.

       Am
The cold, cold ground,
          C
The cold, cold ground,
       Am
The cold, cold ground.

Verse 3

          C   Am
There's a ribbon in the willow, there's a tyre swing rope,

    C   Am
And a briar patch of berries taking over the slope.

     C   Am
The cat'll sleep in the mailbox and we'll never go to town,

     F   G   C
Till we bury every dream in the cold, cold ground.

         Am
In the cold, cold ground

        C
The cold, cold ground,

         Am
In the cold, cold ground,

         C
In the cold, cold ground.

Instrumental

C	Am	C	Am	
C	Am	F	G	‖
‖: C	C	Am	Am	:‖

Verse 4

         C   Am
Gimme a Winchester rifle and a whole box of shells,

C   Am
Blow the roof off the goat barn, let it roll down the hill.

      C   G
The pi - ano is firewood, Times Square is a dream,

    F   G   C
Well I find we'll lay down together in the   cold, cold ground.

         Am
In the cold, cold ground,

      C
Cold cold ground,

         Am
In the cold, cold ground.

Verse 5

          C
We'll call the cops on the Breedloves,

    Am
Bring a bible and a rope,

    C   **Am**
And a whole box of Rebel and a bar of soap.

    C   **Am**
Make a pile of trunk tyres and burn 'em all down,

F   **G**   **C**
Bring a dollar with you baby in the cold cold ground.

    Am
In the cold, cold ground,

      C
In the cold, cold ground,

    Am
In the cold, cold ground.

Verse 6

    C   **Am**
Take a weathervane rooster, throw rocks at his head,

    C   **Am**
Stop talking to the neighbours un - til we all go dead.

    C   **Am**
Be - ware of my temper and the dog that I've found,

F   **G**   **C**
Break all the windows in the cold cold ground,

    Am
In the cold, cold ground.

Outro

         C
‖: In the cold, cold ground,

    Am
In the cold, cold ground.:‖ *Repeat to fade*

Christmas Card From A Hooker In Minneapolis

Words & Music by Tom Waits

F♯ A♯7 B7 C♯11 G♯m7 A♯m7 B C♯7 D♯m7 F♯7/E D♯m7/C♯

Intro

| F♯ | A♯7 | B7 | F♯ | A♯7 | B7 C♯11 |

| F♯ | A♯7 | B7 | G♯m7 | A♯m7 | B C♯11 ‖

Verse 1

F♯
Hey Charlie, I'm pregnant and living on 9th street,
F♯   A♯7   B7
Right above a dirty bookstore   off Euclid avenue.
F♯   A♯7   B7
I stopped taking dope and I quit drinking whiskey,
        G♯m7   A♯m7   B   C♯11 F♯   C♯11
And my old man plays the trombone and works out at the track.

Verse 2

F♯   A♯7   B7
He says that he loves me,   even though it's not his baby,
F♯   A♯7   B7
He says that he'll raise him up like he would his own son.
F♯   A♯7   D♯m7   F♯7/E
He gave me a ring that was worn by his mother,
        B7   C♯11   B   C♯11 F♯   C♯7
And he takes me out dancing every Satur - day   night.

Verse 3

F♯   A♯7   B7
Hey Charlie, I think about you   everytime I pass a filling station,
F♯   A♯7   B7
On account of all the grease you used to wear in your hair.
F♯   A♯7   D♯m7   F♯7/E
I still have that record of Little Anthony And The Imperials,
        B7   C♯11   F♯ A♯7
But someone stole my record player, how do you like that?

Bridge

D♯m7   D♯m7/C♯   G♯m7   A♯m7
Hey Charlie, I almost went crazy   after Mario got busted,
B7   C♯11   F♯   A♯7
I went back to Omaha to live with my folks.
D♯m7   D♯m7/C♯   B7
But everyone I used to know was either dead or in prison,
G♯m7   A♯m7   B7   C♯11 C♯7
So I came back to Minneapolis, this time I think I'm gonna stay.

Verse 4

F♯   A♯7   B7
Hey Charlie, I think I'm happy   for the first time since my accident,
F♯   A♯7   B7
I wish I had all the money we used to spend on dope.
F♯   A♯7   D♯m7   F♯7/E
I'd buy me a used car lot and I wouldn't sell any of 'em,
      B7   C♯11   B7   C♯11 F♯ C♯7
I'd just   drive a different car every day de - pending on how I feel.

Verse 5

F♯   A♯7   B7
Hey Charlie,   for chrissakes,   do you want to know the truth of it?
F♯   A♯7   B7
I don't have a husband,   he don't play the trombone.
F♯   A♯7   D♯m7   F♯7/E
I need to borrow money to pay this lawyer and Charlie, hey,
     B7   C♯11   F♯
I'll be eligible for parole come Valentine's Day.

Clap Hands

Words & Music by Tom Waits

Intro

| Bm | Bm | Bm | Bm |

| G7 | Bm | G7 | Bm |

Verse 1

Bm
Sane, sane, they're all insane,

Fireman's blind, the conductor is lame.

A Cincinnati jacket and a sad-luck dame,

Hanging out the window with a bottle full of rain.
G7   Bm   G7   Bm
Clap hands, clap hands, clap hands, clap hands.

Verse 2

Bm
Said roar, roar, the thunder and the roar,

Son of a bitch is never coming back here no more.

The moon in the window and a bird on the pole,

We can always find a millionaire to shovel all the coal.
G7   Bm   G7   Bm
Clap hands, clap hands, clap hands, clap hands.

Bridge 1

      G7   **Bm**
Said steam, steam, a hundred bad dreams,
G7   **Bm**
Going up to Harlem with a pistol in his jeans.
  G7   **Bm**
A fifty-dollar bill inside a Paladin's hat,
    G7
And nobody's sure where Mr. Knickerbocker's at.

Verse 3

Bm
Roar, roar, the thunder and the roar,

Son of a bitch is never coming back here no more.

Moon in the window and a bird on the pole,

Always find a millionaire to shovel all the coal.
    G7   **Bm**   **G7**   **Bm**
Clap hands, clap hands, clap hands, clap hands.

Guitar solo

| **Bm** | **Bm** | **Bm** | **Bm** |
| **G7** | **Bm** | **G7** | **Bm** |

Bridge 2   As Bridge 1

Verse 4

Bm
Shine, shine, a Roosevelt dime,

All the way to Baltimore and running out of time.

Salvation Army seemed to wind up in the hole,

They all went to Heaven in a little row boat.
    G7   **Bm**   **G7**   **Bm**
Clap hands, clap hands, clap hands, clap hands.
    G7   **Bm**   **G7**   **Bm**
Clap hands, clap hands, clap hands, clap hands.
    G7   **Bm**   **G7**   **Bm**
Clap hands, clap hands, clap hands, clap hands.   *To fade*

Come On Up To The House

Words & Music by Tom Waits & Kathleen Brennan

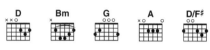

Capo first fret

Intro | D Bm | G D | D A | D ‖

Verse 1
 D   Bm
Well the moon is broken,

   G   D
And the sky is cracked,

   D/F# Bm
Come on up to the house.

     D
The only things that you can see,

  G   D
Is all that you lack,

     A   D
Come on up to the house.

Verse 2
 D   Bm   G   D
All your crying don't do no good,

        Bm
Come on up to the house.

   D   Bm
Come down off the cross,

   G   D
We can use the wood,

        A   D
You got to come on up to the house.

Chorus 1
 D
Come on up to the house,

        Bm
Come on up to the house.

cont.

        D   **Bm**
The world is not my home,

      G   **D**
I'm just a - passing through,

        A   **D**
You got to come on up to the house.

Link 1 | **D A** | **D** ‖

      D   **Bm**
Verse 3 There's no light in the tunnel,

     G   **D**
No irons in the fire,

        Bm
Come on up to the house.

         D
And you're singing lead soprano,

     G   **D**
In a junkman's choir,

        A   **D**
You got to come on up to the house.

      D   **Bm** **G**   **D**
Verse 4 Does life seem nasty, brutish and short?

        Bm
Come on up to the house.

      D   **Bm**
The seas are stormy,

      G   **D**
And you can't find no port,

      A   **D**
Got to come on up to the house.

Chorus 2 As Chorus 1

Instrumental | **D Bm** | **G D** | **D** | **Bm** |

                 | **D Bm** | **G D** | **D A** | **D** ‖

Chorus 3 As Chorus 1

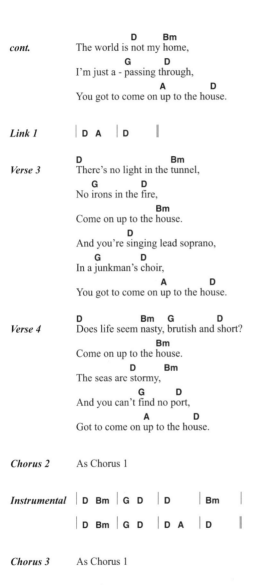

Verse 5

    D   Bm
There's nothing in the world,

    G   D
That you can do,

                       Bm
You got to come on up to the house.

              D   Bm
And you been whipped by the forces,

       G   D
That are inside you,

              A   D
Got to come on up to the house.

Verse 6

    D   Bm
Well, you're high on top,

       G   D
Of your mountain of woe,

                 Bm
Got to come on up to the house.

        D   Bm
Well you know you should sur - render,

       G   D
But you can't let go,

              A   D
You got to come on up to the house.

Chorus 4

    D
Got to come on up to the house,

                   Bm
Got to come on up to the house.

          D   Bm
The world is not my home,

          G   D
I'm just a - passing through,

             A   D
You got to come on up to the house.

             A   D
Got to come on up to the house.

             A   G
You got to come on up to the house.

          D
Oh yeah.____

Day After Tomorrow

Words & Music by Tom Waits & Kathleen Brennan

C	G7	Csus4	Am	F

Intro | C | G7 | C | Csus4 | C ‖

Verse 1

Csus4   C   Csus4 C Csus4
I got your letter to - day,

        C   G7
And I miss you oh so much here.

           Am   C
I can't wait to see you all,

Am   C   G7
And I'm counting the days dear.

           F   C
I still be - lieve that there's gold,

                F
At the end of the world,

               C   Csus4 C
And I'll come home to Illinois,

Am   C   G7   C   Csus4 C Csus4
On the day after to - mor - row.

Verse 2

Csus4 C   Csus4   C   Csus4
It is so hard   and it's cold here,

           C   G7
And I'm tired of taking orders.

           Am   C
And I miss old Rockford town,

      Am   C   G7
Up by the Wis - consin border.

F   C
What I miss you won't be - lieve,

                      F
Shoveling snow, and raking leaves.

       C   Csus4   C
And my plane will touch down,

Csus4 C   G7   C   Csus4 C Csus4
On the day after to - mor - row.

Verse 3

Csus4   C   Csus4   C
I close my eyes every night,

Csus4 C   G7
And I   dream that I can hold you.

                  Am   C
They fill us full of lies everyone buys,

Am   C   G7
'Bout what it means to be a soldier.

                F   C
I still don't know how I'm supposed to feel,

                        F
'Bout all the blood that's been spilled.

                C   Csus4   C
Will God on his throne get me back home,

Csus4 C   G7   C   Csus4 C Csus4
On the day after to - mor - row?

Verse 4

Csus4   C Csus4   C
You can't de - ny the other side,

Csus4   C   G7
Don't wanna die anymore than we do.

                  Am   C
What I'm trying to say is don't they pray,

Am   C   G7
To the same God that we do?

           F   C
Tell me how does God choose?

                      F
Whose prayers does He re - fuse?

             C   Csus4   C
Who turns the wheel, who   throws the dice,

Csus4 C   G7   C   Csus4 C Csus4
On the day after to - mor - row?

C   F C
Mmm,___ mmm.

 F   C   G7
Mmm, mmm, mmm.

Verse 5

  G7   C   Csus4   C
I am not fighting   for justice,

Csus4 C   G7
I am not fighting for freedom.

       Am   C
I am fighting for my life,

Am   C   G7
And another day in the world here.

      F   C
I just do what I've been told,

                  F
We're just the gravel on the road.

        C   Csus4   C
And only the lucky ones come home,

Csus4   C   G7   C   Csus4 C Csus4
  On the day after to - mor - row.

Verse 6

Csus4 C   Csus4   C
And the summer it too will fade,

Csus4   C   G7
And with it brings the winter's frost, dear.

       Am   C
And I know we too are made,

     Am   C   G7
Of all the things that we have lost here.

      F   C
I'll be twenty-one to - day,

                  F
I been saving all my pay.

      C   Csus4   C
And my plane will touch down,

Csus4 C   G7   C   Csus4 C
On the day after to - mor - row.

Csus4 C   Csus4   C
And my plane, it will touch down,

Csus4 C   G7   C   Csus4 C
On the day after to - mor - row.

Dirt In The Ground

Words & Music by Tom Waits & Kathleen Brennan

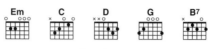

Capo first fret

Intro | Em C | D Em | Em C | D Em ‖

Verse 1

Em   C   Em   C
   What does it matter, a dream of love or a dream of lies,

D   G   B7
   We're all gonna be in the same place when we die.

Em   C   Em   C
   Your spirit don't leave knowing   your face or your name,

D   G   B7
   Wind through your bones is all that re - mains.

Chorus 1

(B7)   Em   C D   Em
And we're all gonna be, yeah, yeah,

                 C D   Em
I said we're all gonna be, yeah, yeah,

                 C D   Em
I said we're all gonna be, yeah, yeah,

I said we're all gonna be just dirt in the ground.

Verse 2

Em   C   Em   C
   The quill   from a buzzard,   the blood writes the word,

D   G   B7
   I want to know am I the sky or a bird?

Em   C   Em   C
   Hell's boiling over   and heaven is full,

     D   G   B7
We're chained to the world and we all got to pull.

Chorus 2   As Chorus 1

Verse 3

    Em   **C**   **Em**   **C**
Now the killer was smiling with nerves made of stone,
D   **G**   **B7**
  He climbed the stairs and the gallows groaned.
      Em   **C**
And the people's hearts were pounding,
       Em   **C**
They were throbbing, they were red,
    D   **G**   **B7**
He swung out over the crowd I heard the hangman said...

Chorus 3   As Chorus 1

Verse 4

     Em   **C** **Em**   **C**
Now Cain slew Abel,   he killed him with a stone,
D   **G**   **B7**
  The sky cracked open   and the thunder groaned.
Em   **C**   **Em**   **C**
Along a river of flesh can these dry bones live?
D   **G**   **B7**
Take a king or a beggar and the answer they'll give.

Chorus 4

(B7)   **Em**   **C** **D**   **Em**
Is we're all gonna be, yeah, yeah,
                 C **D**   **Em**
I said we're all gonna be, yeah, yeah,
                 C **D**   **Em**
I said we're all gonna be, yeah, yeah,

I said we're all gonna be just dirt in the ground.
            C   **D**   **Em**
We're all gonna be just dirt in the ground.
            C   **D**   **Em**
We're all gonna be just dirt in the ground.
            C   **D**   **Em**
I said we're all gonna be just dirt in the ground.
            C   **D**   **Em**
Yeah, we're all gonna be just dirt in the ground.

Downtown Train

Words & Music by Tom Waits

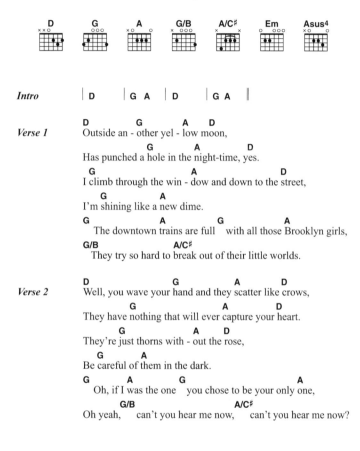

Intro | D | G A | D | G A ||

Verse 1

D   G   A   D
Outside an - other yel - low moon,

              G   A   D
Has punched a hole in the night-time, yes.

G   A   D
I climb through the win - dow and down to the street,

     G   A
I'm shining like a new dime.

G   A   G   A
  The downtown trains are full   with all those Brooklyn girls,

G/B   A/C#
  They try so hard to break out of their little worlds.

Verse 2

D   G   A   D
Well, you wave your hand and they scatter like crows,

              G   A   D
They have nothing that will ever capture your heart.

        G   A   D
They're just thorns with - out the rose,

     G   A
Be careful of them in the dark.

G   A   G   A
  Oh, if I was the one   you chose to be your only one,

          G/B   A/C#
Oh yeah,   can't you hear me now,   can't you hear me now?

Chorus 1

D   G   D   G
Will I see you to - night   on a downtown train?

D   G   Em
Every night it's just the same,

A   D
You leave me lonely now.

Verse 3

D   G   A   D
I know your window and I know it's late,

        G   A   D
I know your stairs and your doorway.

                G   A   D
I walk down your street and past your gate,

            G   A
I stand by the light at the four-way.

G   A
You watch them as they fall,

  G   A
Oh baby, they all have heart at - tacks,

     G/B   A/C♯
They stay at the carnival, but they'll never win you back.

Chorus 2

D   G   D   G
Will I see you to - night   on a downtown train?

D   G   Em   A
Where every night,   every night it's just the same,   oh baby.

D   G   D   G
Will I see you to - night   on a downtown train?

D   G   Em
All of my dreams they fall like rain,

    A   (D)
Oh baby on a downtown train.

Guitar solo | D   A | D   A | D   G | A |

               | D   A | D   A | D   G | A | Asus⁴ ‖

Chorus 3

D   G   D   G
   Will I see you to - night   on a downtown train?

D   G   Em   A
Where every night, every night it's just the same, oh baby.

D   G   D   G
   Will I see you to - night   on a downtown train?

D   G   Em
   All of my dreams just fall like rain,

A   D
   All on a downtown train,

G   A   D   G   A   D
   All on a downtown train,   all on a downtown train,

G   A   D   G   A   (D)
   All on a downtown train,   a downtown train.

Outro

| D | G A | D | G A |

| D | G A | D | |

52

Dead And Lovely

Words & Music by Tom Waits & Kathleen Brennan

Cm   A♭7   G7   Fm   D♭7   D7

Intro
| Cm | Cm | Cm | Cm |

| Cm | A♭7 G7 | Cm ‖

Verse 1

Cm
She was a middle-class girl, she was in over her head,
Fm   Cm
   She thought she could stand up in the deep end.

He had a bulletproof smile, he had money to burn,
Fm   Cm
   She thought she had the moon in her pocket.

Chorus 1

Cm   A♭7
But now she's dead,

        Cm A♭7
She's so dead,

        Cm   A♭7   G7 Cm
Forever dead and love - ly now.

Bridge 1

Fm D♭7   Fm   D♭7
I've   always been told to re - member this,
Cm   A♭7   D7   G7
   Don't let a fool kiss you,   never marry for love.

Verse 2

(G7)   Cm
He was hard to im - press, he knew everyone's secrets,
Fm   Cm
   He wore her on his arm just like jewellery.

He never gave but he got, he kept her on a leash,
Fm   Cm
   He's not the kind of wheel you fall asleep at.

Chorus 2   As Chorus 1

Fm   **D♭7**   **Fm**   **D♭7**
Bridge 2   Come closer,   look deeper,   you're falling fast,
Cm   **A♭7**   **D7**   **G7**
              Just like a   plane on a   stormy sea.

(G7)   **Cm**
Verse 3   She made up someone to be,

             She made up somewhere to be from,
             Fm
                This is one business in the world,
                          Cm
             Where there's no problem at all.

             Everything that is left they will only plow under,
             Fm   **Cm**
                Soon everyone you knew will be gone.

             Cm   **A♭7**
Chorus 3   And now she's dead,
                      Cm   **A♭7**
             Forever   dead,
                      Cm   **A♭7** **G7** **Cm**
             Forever dead and love - ly   now.

Instrumental ‖: **Cm** | **Cm** | **Cm** | **Cm** |

                | **Fm** | **Fm** | **Cm** | **Cm**   :‖

             Cm   **A♭7**
Chorus 4   But now she's dead,
                       Cm   **A♭7**
             Forever dead,
                       Cm   **A♭7** **G7** **Cm**
             Forever dead and love - ly   now.

             Fm **D♭7**   **Fm**   **D♭7**
Bridge 3   I've   always been told to re - member this,
             Cm   **A♭7**   **D7**   **G7**
                Don't let a   kiss fool you,   never marry for love.

Verse 4

(G7)   **Cm**
Everything has it's price, everything has it's place,

Fm   **Cm**
  What's more romantic than dying in the moonlight?

Now they're all watching the sea,

What's lost can never be broken,

Fm   **Cm**
  Her roots were sweet but they were so shallow.

Chorus 5   As Chorus 3

Chorus 6

Cm   **A♭7**
And now she's dead,

         Cm   **A♭7**
Forever dead,

              Cm   **A♭7**   **G7** **Cm**
And she's so dead and love - ly now.

Falling Down

Words & Music by Tom Waits

Capo first fret

Intro

| C | Am | Gsus⁴ | G | |

| C | Am | B♭ | Gsus⁴ G ‖

Verse 1

(G)   C   Am   Gsus⁴   G
I've come five hundred miles just to see a ha - lo,

C   Am   B♭   Gsus⁴
Come from St. Petersburg, Scarlett and me.

G   C   Am   Gsus⁴ G
Well I open my eyes, I was blind as can be,

           C   Am   B♭   Gsus⁴
When you give a man luck, he must fall in the sea.

        Dm   Dm/C   G/B   G
And she wants you to steal and get caught,

        Dm   Dm/C   G/B   G
For she loves you for all that you are not.

             C   Am   Gsus⁴ G
When you're falling down,   falling down.

                    C   Am   Gsus⁴ G
When you're falling down, fall - ing down, falling down.

Verse 2

(N.C.)   C   Am   Gsus⁴   G
You for - get all the roses, don't come around on Sunday,

           C   Am   B♭   Gsus⁴
She's not gonna choose you for standing so tall.

G   C   Am   Gsus⁴   G
  Go on and take a swig of that poison and like it,

             C   Am   B♭   Gsus⁴
And now don't ask for silverware, don't ask for nothing.

cont.

        Dm   Dm/C   G/B   G
Go on and put your ear to the ground,

                       Dm   Dm/C Gsus⁴   G
You know you will be hearing that sound,   falling down.

              C Am   Gsus⁴ G
You're falling down,   fall - ing   down.

                C Am   Gsus⁴ G N.C. (C)
Falling down,   falling down,   falling down.

Guitar solo

C	Am	Gsus⁴	G	
C	Am	B♭	Gsus⁴ G	
C	Am	Gsus⁴	G	
C	Am	B♭	Gsus⁴ G	
Dm	Dm/C	G/B	G	
Dm	Dm/C	Gsus⁴	G	

(G)   C   Am   Gsus⁴ G   C   Am   Gsus⁴ G
When you're falling down,   falling down, falling down.

Verse 3

N.C. C   Am   Gsus⁴   G
Go on down and see that wrecking ball come swinging on along,

C   Am   B♭   Gsus⁴
Everyone knew that ho - tel was a goner.

G C   Am   Gsus⁴   G
They broke all the windows, they took all the door knobs,

            C   Am   B♭   Gsus⁴
And they hauled it a - way in a couple of days.

Dm   Dm/C   G/B   G
  Now someone yell timber and take off your hat,

       Dm   Dm/C   Gsus⁴
They all look smaller down here on the ground.

G   C   Am   Gsus⁴   G
  When you're fall - ing down,   falling down, falling down.

      C   Am   Gsus⁴ G N.C. C   Am
Falling down, falling down,   falling down.

Gsus⁴   G   C   Am   Gsus⁴ G C   Am
Someone's falling down,   falling down, fall - ing down.

       Gsus⁴ G   C   Am Gsus⁴ G Dm⁷   G C
Falling down, fall - ing down,   fall - ing down.

Fannin Street

Words & Music by Tom Waits & Kathleen Brennan

C/G   F   G7   Csus4/G   C
E   Am   D7   G/B   Fsus2

Intro
| C/G | C/G | C/G ‖

Verse 1

C/G   F   G7   C/G   Csus4/G C/G
There's a crooked street in Houston town,

      F   G7   C/G   Csus4/G C/G
It's a well-worn path I've travelled down.

           F   G7   C   E   Am
Now there's ruin in my name, I wish I'd never got off the train,

       D7   G7   C/G Csus4/G C/G
And I wished I'd listened to the words you said.

Chorus 1

C/G   Csus4/G   C/G   Csus4/G C/G
Don't go down   to Fannin Street,

        F   C/G   Csus4/G C/G
Don't go down to Fannin Street,

        F   C   G/B Am
Don't go down to Fannin Street,   oh yeah,

       C/G   Fsus2
You'll be lost and never found.

       C/G   Fsus2
You can never turn around,

         C/G   G7   C/G   Csus4/G C/G
Don't go down to   Fannin Street.

Verse 2

```
C/G    F                    G7           C/G    Csus4/G  C/G
Once I held you in my arms, I was sure,
               F             G7              C/G    Csus4/G  C/G
Then I took that silent step through the gilded door.
            F                 G7           C      E       Am
The de - sire to have much more, all the glitter and the roar,
        D7        G7                    C/G    Csus4/G  C/G
Now I know just where the sidewalk ends.
```

Chorus 2   As Chorus 1

Verse 3

```
C/G        F                  G7          C/G    Csus4/G  C/G
When I was young I thought only of getting out,
               F          G7              C/G    Csus4/G  C/G
I said good - bye to my street, goodbye to my house.
               F              G7            C      E       Am
Give a man gin, give a man cards, give him an inch, he takes a yard,
        D7            G7              C/G    Csus4/G  C/G
And I rue the day that I stepped off this train.
```

Chorus 3   As Chorus 1

Chorus 4   As Chorus 1

Outro

```
C/G              G7      C/G    Csus4/G  C/G
Don't go down to   Fannin Street.
                 G7      C/G    Csus4/G  C/G
Don't go down to   Fannin Street.
```

Fumblin' With The Blues

Words & Music by Tom Waits

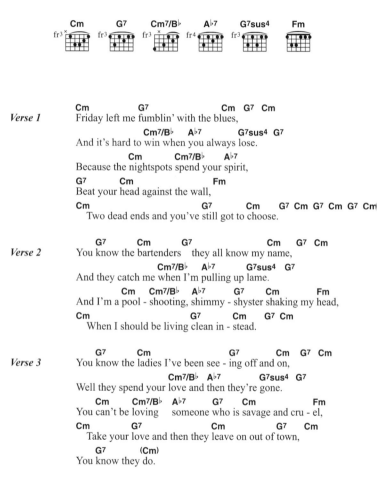

Verse 1

    Cm   G7   Cm G7 Cm
Friday left me fumblin' with the blues,

             Cm7/B♭   A♭7   G7sus4 G7
And it's hard to win when you always lose.

           Cm   Cm7/B♭   A♭7
Because the nightspots spend your spirit,

G7   Cm   Fm
Beat your head against the wall,

Cm   G7   Cm   G7 Cm G7 Cm G7 Cm
   Two dead ends and you've still got to choose.

Verse 2

      G7   Cm   G7   Cm   G7 Cm
You know the bartenders   they all know my name,

               Cm7/B♭   A♭7   G7sus4 G7
And they catch me when I'm pulling up lame.

           Cm Cm7/B♭ A♭7   G7   Cm   Fm
And I'm a pool - shooting, shimmy - shyster shaking my head,

Cm   G7   Cm   G7 Cm
   When I should be living clean in - stead.

Verse 3

      G7   Cm   G7   Cm G7 Cm
You know the ladies I've been see - ing off and on,

              Cm7/B♭ A♭7   G7sus4 G7
Well they spend your love and then they're gone.

      Cm   Cm7/B♭   A♭7   G7   Cm   Fm
You can't be loving   someone who is savage and cru - el,

Cm   G7   Cm   G7   Cm
   Take your love and then they leave on out of town,

     G7   (Cm)
You know they do.

Instr. | Cm G7 | Cm G7 Cm | Cm Cm7/B♭ A♭ | G7sus4 G7 |

| Cm Cm7/B♭ A♭ G7 | Cm Fm | Cm G7 | Cm G7 Cm G7 ‖

Verse 4

(G7)   Cm   G7   Cm G7 Cm
Well now falling in love   is such a breeze,

                 Cm7/B♭ A♭7   G7sus4 G7
But it's standing up that's so hard for me.

        Cm   Cm7/B♭ A♭7   G7   Cm   Fm
I wanna squeeze you but I'm scared to death I'd break your back,

Cm   G7   Cm G7 Cm
   You know your per - fume, well it won't let me be.

Verse 5

         G7   Cm   G7   Cm G7 Cm
And you know the bartenders all know my name,

               Cm7/B♭   A♭7   G7sus4 G7
And they catch me when I'm pulling up lame.

        Cm   Cm7/B♭ A♭7   G7   Cm   Fm
And I'm a pool - shooting, shimmy - shyster shaking my head,

Cm   G7   Cm   G7 Cm
   When I should be living clean in - stead.

Verse 6

        G7 Cm G7   Cm G7 Cm
Come on baby,   let your love-light shine,

              Cm7/B♭ A♭7   G7sus4 G7
Got to bury me in - side of your fire.

        Cm   Cm7/B♭   A♭7
Because your eyes are enough to blind me,

G7   Cm   Fm
You're like a - looking at the sun,

Cm   G7   Cm G7 Cm
   You got to whisper tell me I'm the one.

        G7   Cm   G7   Cm G7 Cm
Come on and whisper tell me I'm the one.

G7   Cm   G7   Cm   G7 Cm
Got to whisper tell me I'm the one.

        G7   Cm   G7sus4 G7   (Cm)
Come on and whisper tell me I'm_____ the one.

Outro | Cm Cm7/B♭ A♭ G7 | Cm Fm | Cm G7 | Cm G7 Cm ‖

Eggs And Sausage
(In A Cadillac With
Susan Michelson)

Words & Music by Tom Waits

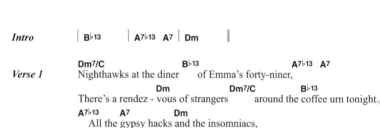

B♭13   A7♭13   A7   Dm   Dm7/C

Intro | B♭13 | A7♭13 A7 | Dm   ‖

Verse 1
Dm7/C   B♭13   A7♭13 A7
Nighthawks at the diner   of Emma's forty-niner,
                         Dm   Dm7/C   B♭13
There's a rendez - vous of strangers   around the coffee urn tonight.
A7♭13   A7   Dm
  All the gypsy hacks and the insomniacs,
Dm7/C   B♭13
Now the paper's been read,
A7♭13   A7   Dm
   Now the waitress said:

Chorus 1
Dm   Dm7/C   B♭13
"Eggs and sausage and a side of toast,
A7♭13   A7 Dm   Dm7/C
Coffee and a roll,   hash browns over easy,
B♭13   A7♭13 A7   Dm   Dm7/C
  Chili in a bowl   with burgers and fries,
                  B♭13
What kind of pie?"

Verse 2

A7♭13 A7 Dm   Dm7/C   B♭13
It's a grave - yard charade, it's a late shift masquerade,

A7♭13   A7   Dm   Dm7/C   B♭13
And it's two for a quarter,   dime for a dance.

A7♭13   A7   Dm
Woolworth rhinestone   diamond earrings,

Dm7/C   B♭13
And a sideways glance.

A7♭13   A7   Dm
And now the register rings,

Dm7/C   B♭13
Now the waitress sings:

Chorus 2

A7♭13   A7 Dm   Dm7/C
"Eggs and sausage and a side of toast,

B♭13   A7♭13 A7   Dm   Dm7/C
Coffee and a roll,   hash browns over ea - sy,

B♭13   A7♭13 A7   Dm
Chili in a bowl,   burgers and fries,

            Dm7/C B♭13 A7♭13 A7
What kind of pie?"

Piano solo   ‖: Dm | Dm7/C | B♭13 | A7♭13 A7 :‖ *Play 4 times*

Verse 3

(A7) Dm   Dm7/C   B♭13   A7♭13 A7
Now well, the classi - fied section   offers no direc - tion,

        Dm   Dm7/C   B♭13
It's a cold caffeine   in a nicotine cloud.

A7♭13   A7   Dm   Dm7/C
Now the touch of your fingers,

          B♭13   A7♭13 A7
Lingers, burning in my memo - ry.

            Dm   Dm7/C
I've been eighty - sixed from your scheme,

          B♭13   A7♭13
Now I'm in a melodramatic nocturnal scene.

A7   Dm   Dm7/C
Now I'm a refugee from a dis - concerted affair.

B♭13   A7♭13   A7
Now the lead pipe morning falls,

Dm Dm7/C   B♭13
Now the waitress calls:

Chorus 3

A7♭13 A7   Dm   Dm7/C   B♭13   A7♭13 A7
      "Eggs and sausage,   now a side of toast,

Dm   Dm7/C   B♭13   A7♭13
    Coffee and a roll,   hash browns over ea - sy,

     A7   Dm   Dm7/C
Chi - li in a bowl with burgers and fries,

       B♭13
Now what kind of pie?"

Verse 3

A7♭13   A7 Dm   Dm7/C
    A la mode,— if you will,

B♭13   A7♭13   A7
    Just coming at you in a crowd.

      Dm   Dm7/C
Had some time to kill,

          B♭13   A7♭13
See I just come in to join the crowd.

A7   Dm
Had some time to kill,

      Dm7/C
Just coming at you in a crowd,

     B♭13   A7♭13   Dm   Dm7/C B♭13 A7♭13 A7 Dm
'Cause I had some time to kill.

God's Away On Business

Words & Music by Tom Waits & Kathleen Brennan

B♭m G♭7 F7 E♭m F♯7 Bm Em G7

Intro

| B♭m | G♭7 F7 | B♭m | G♭7 | |

| B♭m | G♭7 | B♭m | G♭7 ‖

Verse 1

B♭m
I'd sell your heart to the junk-man baby,

For a buck, for a buck!

E♭m
If you're looking for someone to pull you out of that ditch,

You're out of luck, you're out of luck.

F7   B♭m   F7   B♭m
Ship is sinking, the ship is sinking,

F7   B♭m
The ship is sinking.

Pre-chorus 1

B♭m   G♭7
There's a leak, there's a leak in the boiler room,

B♭m   G♭7
The poor, the lame, the blind.

B♭m   G♭7
Who are the ones that we kept in charge?

B♭m   G♭7
Killers, thieves and lawyers.

Chorus 1

B♭m
God's away, God's away,

God's away on business, business.

God's away, God's away,

F#7
God's away on business, business.

Verse 2

Bm
Digging up the dead with a shovel and a pick,

It's a job, it's a job.
Em
Bloody moon rising with a plague and a flood,

Join the mob, join the mob.
F#7   Bm   F#7   Bm F#7   Bm
It's all over, it's all over, it's all over.

Pre-chorus 2

Bm   G7
There's a leak, there's a leak in the boiler room,

Bm   G7
The poor, the lame, the blind.
Bm   G7
Who are the ones that we kept in charge?
Bm   G7
Killers, thieves and lawyers.

Chorus 2

Bm
God's away, God's away,

God's away on business, business.

God's away, God's away on business, business.

Instrumental ‖: Bm | G7 | Bm | G7 :‖

| Bm | Bm | Bm | Bm ‖

66

	Bm G7
Bridge 1	Goddam, there's always such a big temptation,

Bm   G7
To be good, to be good.

Bm   G7
There's always free cheddar in the mousetrap, baby,

Bm   G7
It's a deal, It's a deal.

Bm

Chorus 3   God's away, God's away,

God's away on business, business.

God's away, God's away,

God's away on business, business.

Bm   G7

Bridge 2   I narrow my eyes like a coin slot, baby,

Bm   G7
Let her ring, let her ring.

Bm

Chorus 4   God's away, God's away,

God's away on business, business.

God's away, God's away,

God's away on business, business.

Goin' Out West

Words & Music by Tom Waits & Kathleen Brennan

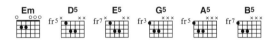

Tune guitar down two tones

Intro	Em	Em	Em	Em
	Em	Em	Em	Em	N.C.
	D5 E5	E5 D5	D5 E5	E5 D5

Verse 1

    D5 E5   D5 Em
I'm go - in' out west where the wind blows tall,

'Cause Tony Franciosa used to date my ma.

They got some money out there, they're giving it away,

I'm gonna do what I want and I'm gonna get paid.

Do what I want and I'm gonna get paid.

Verse 2

D5 E5   D5 E5
Lit - tle brown sausages lying in the sand,
    D5 E5   D5 E5
I ain't no ex - tra baby, I'm a leading man.
     D5 E5   Em
Well my pa - role officer will be proud of me,

With my Olds '88 and the devil on a leash,
    D5 E5
My Olds '88 and the devil on a leash.

	G5 A5 **G5 A5**
Chorus 1	Well, I know karate, voo - doo too,

               D5   E5   **D5   E5**
               I'm gon - na make myself avail - able to you.

               G5   A5   **G5   A5**
               I don't need no make up, I got real   scars,

               B5
               I got   hair on my chest,

               I look good without a shirt.

	Em
Verse 3	Well, I don't lose my composure in a high speed chase,

               Well, my friends think I'm ugly, I got a masculine face.

               I got some dragstrip courage, I can really drive em' dead,

               I'm gonna change my name to Hannibal, maybe just Rex,

               Change my name to Hannibal, maybe just Rex.

| *Chorus 2* | As Chorus 1 |

	Em
Verse 4	I'm gonna drive all night, hit some speed,

               I'm gonna wait for the sun to shine down on me.

               I cut a hole in my roof the shape of a heart,

               And I'm goin' out west where they'll appreciate me.

               I'm goin' out west where they'll appreciate me.

               I'm goin' out west where they'll appreciate me.

               I'm goin' out west where they'll appreciate me.

	Em
Outro	Goin' out west, goin' out west. *Repeat to fade*

Hang Down Your Head

Words & Music by Tom Waits & Kathleen Brennan

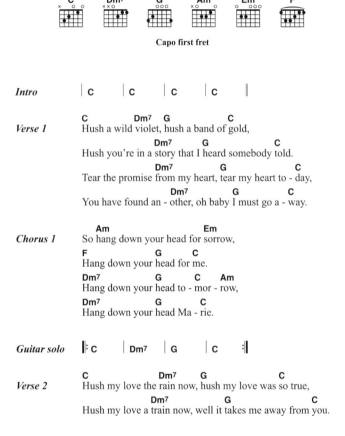

Capo first fret

Intro

| C | C | C | C |

Verse 1

C   Dm7   G   C
Hush a wild violet, hush a band of gold,

             Dm7   G   C
Hush you're in a story that I heard somebody told.

             Dm7   G   C
Tear the promise from my heart, tear my heart to - day,

             Dm7   G   C
You have found an - other, oh baby I must go a - way.

Chorus 1

      Am   Em
So hang down your head for sorrow,

F   G   C
Hang down your head for me.

Dm7   G   C   Am
Hang down your head to - mor - row,

Dm7   G   C
Hang down your head Ma - rie.

Guitar solo

‖: C | Dm7 | G | C :‖

Verse 2

C   Dm7   G   C
Hush my love the rain now, hush my love was so true,

             Dm7   G   C
Hush my love a train now, well it takes me away from you.

Chorus 2

      Am   **Em**
So hang down your head for sorrow,

F   **G**   **C**
Hang down your head for me.

Dm7   **G**   **C**   **Am**
Hang down your head, hang down your head,

Dm7   **G**   **C**
Hang down your head Ma - rie.

Chorus 3   As Chorus 2

Outro   ‖: C | C | C | C   :‖ C |

Hang On St. Christopher

Words & Music by Tom Waits

Intro | D5 | D5 | D5 | D5   ‖

Verse 1

D5
Hang on St. Christopher through the smoke and the oil,

Buckle down the rumble seat, let the radiator boil.

G5
   Got an overhead downshift and a two-dollar grill,

D5
   Got an eighty-five cabin on an eighty-five hill.

A5   G5
   Hang on St. Christopher on the passenger side,

D5
   Open it up, tonight the devil can ride.

Verse 2

D5
Hang on St. Christopher with a barrel house dog,

Kick me up Mount Baldy, throw me out in the fog.

G5
   Tear a hole in the jackpot, drive a stake through his heart,

D5
   Do a hundred on the grapevine, do a jump on the start.

A5   G5
   Hang on St. Christopher, now don't let me go,

D5
   Get me to Reno and bring it in low, yeah.

Instr.		D5		D5		D5		D5	
		G5		G5		D5		D5	
		A5		G5		D5		D5	

Verse 3

D5
Hang on St. Christopher with the hammer to the floor,

Put a hi-ball in the crank case, nail a crow to the door.
G5
   Get a bottle for the jockey, get me a two-ninety-four,
D5
   There's a seven-fifty Norton busting down January's door.
A5   **G5**
   Hang on St. Christopher on the passenger side,
D5
   Open it up, tonight the devil can ride.

Verse 4

D5
Hang on St. Christopher now don't let me go,

Get to me Reno, got to bring it in low.
      G5
Put my baby on the flat car got to burn down the caboose,
      D5
Get 'em all jacked up on whiskey then we'll turn the mad dog loose.
A5   **G5**
   Hang on St. Christopher on the passenger side,
D5
   Open it up, tonight the devil can ride, yeah.

Outro	‖: D5		D5		D5		D5	:‖ *Play 3 times*

Heartattack And Vine

Words & Music by Tom Waits

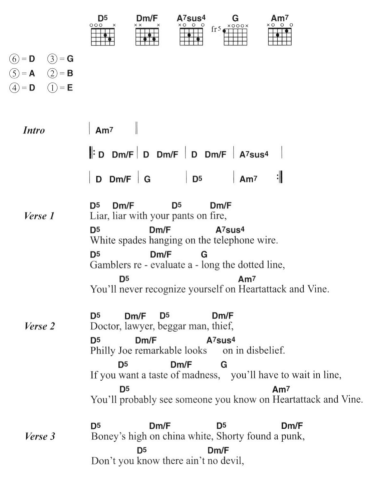

D5   Dm/F   A7sus4   G   Am7

⑥ = D   ③ = G
⑤ = A   ② = B
④ = D   ① = E

Intro | Am7   ‖

‖: D Dm/F | D Dm/F | D Dm/F | A7sus4 |

| D Dm/F | G | D5 | Am7   :‖

Verse 1
D5   Dm/F   D5   Dm/F
Liar, liar with your pants on fire,
D5   Dm/F   A7sus4
White spades hanging on the telephone wire.
D5   Dm/F   G
Gamblers re - evaluate a - long the dotted line,
            D5   Am7
You'll never recognize yourself on Heartattack and Vine.

Verse 2
D5   Dm/F   D5   Dm/F
Doctor, lawyer, beggar man, thief,
D5   Dm/F   A7sus4
Philly Joe remarkable looks   on in disbelief.
            D5   Dm/F   G
If you want a taste of madness,   you'll have to wait in line,
            D5   Am7
You'll probably see someone you know on Heartattack and Vine.

Verse 3
D5   Dm/F   D5   Dm/F
Boney's high on china white, Shorty found a punk,
            D5   Dm/F
Don't you know there ain't no devil,

       A⁷sus⁴

cont.   There's just God when he's drunk,

      D⁵   **Dm/F**
   Well this stuff will probably kill you,

      G
   Let's do another line,

   D⁵   **Am⁷**
   What you say you meet me down on Heartattack and Vine.

Instrumental | D Dm/F | D Dm/F | D Dm/F | A⁷sus⁴ |

     | D Dm/F | G | D⁵ | Am⁷ ||

     D⁵   **Dm/F**   **D⁵**   **Dm/F**
Verse 4 See that little Jersey girl in the see-through top,

       D⁵   **Dm/F**   **A⁷sus⁴**
   With the peddle-pushers sucking on a soda pop,

     D⁵   **Dm/F**
   Well I bet she's still a virgin,

      G
   But it's only twenty-five till nine,

   D⁵   **Am⁷**
   You can see a million of 'em on Heartattack and Vine.

     D⁵   **Dm/F** **D⁵**   **Dm/F**
Verse 5 Better off in Iowa a - gainst your scram - bled eggs,

      D⁵   **Dm/F** **A⁷sus⁴**
   Than crawling down Ca - huenga on a broken pair of legs.

        D⁵   **Dm/F**   **G**
   You'll find your ignorance is blissful every goddam time,

      D⁵   **Am⁷**
   You're waiting for the R.T.D. on Heartattack and Vine.

Verse 6 As Verse 3

Verse 7 As Verse 1

Verse 8 As Verse 2

Verse 9 As Verse 4

Verse 10 As Verse 3 *To fade*

Hoist That Rag

Words & Music by Tom Waits & Kathleen Brennan

Intro ‖: Am Dm │ E7 Am │ Am7 Dm │ B7 E7 :‖

Verse 1
> Am   Dm   E7   Am
> Well, I learned the trade from Piggy Noles,
>
> Am7   Dm   B7   E7
> Sing, sing, Tommy Shay, boys.
>
> Am   Dm   E7   Am
> God used me as a hammer boys,
>
>   Am7   Dm   B7   E7
> To beat his weary drum to - day.

Chorus 1
> (E7)   Am   Dm E7 Am
> Hoist that rag,
>
>   Dm E7 Am
> Hoist that rag,
>
>   Dm E7 Am Dm E7 Am
> Hoist that rag.

Verse 2
>   Am   Dm   E7   Am
> The sun is up, the world is flat,
>
> Am7   Dm   B7   E7
> Damn good address for a rat.
>
>   Am   Dm   E7   Am
> The smell of blood, the drone of flies,
>
>   Am7   Dm   B7   E7
> You know what to do if the baby cries.

Chorus 2

(E7)   **Am Dm E7 Am**
Hoist that rag,

                    Dm
Hoist that rag.

E7   **Am**   **Dm**
   Hoist that rag, hoist that rag.

E7   **Am**   **Dm**
   Hoist that rag, hoist that rag.

E7   **Am**
   Hoist that rag.

Guitar solo   ‖: **Am Dm** | **E7 Am** | **Am Dm** | **E7 Am** :‖ *Play 9 times*

Verse 3

          Am   **Dm**   **E7**   **Am**
Well, we stick our fingers in the ground,

Am7   **Dm**   **B7**   **E7**
Heave and turn the world a - round,

Am   **Dm**   **E7**   **Am**
Smoke has blackened out the sun,

    Am7   **Dm**   **B7**   **E7**
At night I pray and clean my gun.

         Am   **Dm**   **E7**   **Am**
And the cracked bell rings as the ghost bird sings,

      Am7   **Dm**   **B7**   **E7**
The gods go begging here.

        Am   **Dm**   **E7**   **Am**
So just open fire when you hit the shore,

Am7 Dm   B7   **E7**
All is fair in love and war.

Chorus 3

(E7)   **Am Dm E7 Am**
Hoist that rag,

              Dm E7 Am
Hoist that rag.

                Dm
Hoist that rag.

Outro   ‖: **E7**   **Am**   **Dm** :‖
       Hoist that rag, hoist that rag.   *Repeat to fade*

Hold On

Words & Music by Tom Waits & Kathleen Brennan

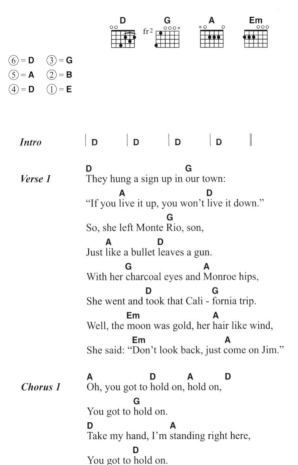

⑥ = D   ③ = G
⑤ = A   ② = B
④ = D   ① = E

Intro | D | D | D | D   ‖

Verse 1

D   G
They hung a sign up in our town:

       A   D
"If you live it up, you won't live it down."

                G
So, she left Monte Rio, son,

      A   D
Just like a bullet leaves a gun.

          G   A
With her charcoal eyes and Monroe hips,

                 D   G
She went and took that Cali - fornia trip.

         Em   A
Well, the moon was gold, her hair like wind,

          Em   A
She said: "Don't look back, just come on Jim."

Chorus 1

A   D   A   D
Oh, you got to hold on, hold on,

          G
You got to hold on.

D   A
Take my hand, I'm standing right here,

          D
You got to hold on.

Verse 2

D   **G**
Well, he gave her a dime-store watch

A   **D**
And a ring made from a spoon.

                      G
Everyone is looking for someone to blame,

         A   **D**
When you share my bed, you share my name.

    G   **A**
Well, go ahead and call the cops,

        D   **G**
You don't meet nice girls in coffee shops.

Em   **A**
She said: "Baby, I still love you,

       Em   **A**
Some - times there's nothing left to do."

Chorus 2

A   **D**   **A**   **D**
Oh, but you got to hold on, hold on,

             G
Baby got to hold on.

    D   **A**
And take a-my hand, I'm standing right here,

      D
You got to hold on.

Verse 3

D   **G**
Well, God bless your crooked little heart,

     A   **D**
St. Louis got the best of me.

              G
I miss your broken - china voice,

      A   **D**
How I wish you were still here with me.

    G   **A**
Oh, you build it up, you wreck it down,

         D   **G**
And you burn your mansion to the ground.

           Em   **A**
Oh, there's nothing left to keep you here,

                Em   **A**
Oh, when you're falling behind in this big blue world.

Chorus 3

 A   D A   D
Oh, you got to hold on, hold on,

     G
Baby got to hold on.

D   A
Take my hand, I'm standing right here,

      D
You got to hold on.

Verse 4

D   G
Now, down by the River - side motel,

  A   D
It's ten below and falling.

      G
By a ninety - nine cent store,

  A   D
She closed her eyes and started swaying.

 G   A
But it's so hard to dance that way,

    D   G
When it's cold and there's no music.

    Em   A
Oh, your old hometown's so far away,

    Em   A
But, in - side your head there's a record that's playing...

Chorus 4

A   D A   D
A song called hold on, hold on,

     G
Baby got to hold on.

D   A
Take my hand, I'm standing right there,

    D
Got to hold on.

Chorus 5

D   A   D
You got to hold on, hold on,

     G
Baby got to hold on.

D   A
Take my hand, I'm standing right there,

    D
You got to hold on.

	D **A** **D**

Chorus 6

    D   **A**   **D**
You got to hold on, hold on,

               G
Baby got to hold on.

              D   **A**
And take my hand, I'm standing right here,

             D
You got to hold on.

Chorus 7

    D   **A**   **D**
You got to hold on, hold on,

               G
Baby got to hold on.

    D   **A**
And take my hand, I'm standing right here,

             D
You got to hold on.

Outro

       D
‖: You got to hold on. :‖ *Play 8 times*

Gun Street Girl

Words & Music by Tom Waits

D5   **A5(7)**

Intro | **D5** | **D5** | **D5** | **D5**   ‖

Verse 1

D5
Falling James in the Tahoe mud,
                              A5(7)
Stick around to tell us all the tale.
            D5
Well he fell in love with a Gun Street girl,

And now he's dancing in the Birmingham jail,

Dancing in the Birmingham jail.

Verse 2

D5
He took a hundred dollars off a slaughterhouse Joe,
                              A5(7)
Bought a brand new Michigan twenty - gauge.
            D5
He got all liquored up on that roadhouse corn,

Blew a hole in the hood of a yellow Corvette,

A hole in the hood of a yellow Corvette.

Verse 3

D5
He bought a second-hand Nova from a Cuban Chinese,
                              A5(7)
And dyed his hair in the bathroom of a Texa - co.
            D5
With a pawnshop radio, quarter past four,

He left for Waukegan at the slamming of the door,

Left for Waukegan at the slamming of the door.

Chorus 1

D5
I said, "John, John, he's long gone,

Gone to Indiana, ain't never coming home."

I said, "John, John, he's long gone,

Gone to Indiana, ain't never coming home."

Verse 4

D5
He's sitting in a sycamore in St. John's Wood,
                    A5(7)
Soaking day-old bread in kero - sene.
     D5
Well he was blue as a robin's egg and brown as a hog,

He's staying out of circulation till the dogs get tired,

Out of circulation till the dogs get tired.

Verse 5

D5
Shadow fixed the toilet with an old trombone,
                        A5(7)
He never get up in the morning on a Satur - day.
D5
Sitting by the Erie with a bull-whipped dog,

Telling everyone he saw, "They went that-a-way, boys."

Telling everyone he saw, "They went that-a-way."

Verse 6

D5
Now the rain's like gravel on an old tin roof,
                     A5(7)
And the Burlington Northern pulling out of the world.
     D5
Now a head full of bourbon and a dream in the straw,

And a Gun Street girl was the cause of it all,

A Gun Street girl was the cause of it all.

Verse 7

D5
Well he's riding in the shadow by the St. Joe ridge,

A5(7)
And the click-clack tapping of a blind man's cane.

D5
He was pulling into Baker on a New Year's Eve,

One eye on the pistol and the other on the door,

One eye on the pistol and the other on the door.

Verse 8

D5
Miss Charlotte took her satchel down to King Fish Row,

A5(7)
Smuggled in a brand new pair of alligator shoes.

D5
With her fireman's raincoat and her long yellow hair,

Well they tied her to a tree with a skinny millionaire,

They tied her to a tree with a skinny millionaire.

Chorus 2   As Chorus 1

Bridge

D5
Banging on the table with an old tin cup,

Sing I'll never kiss a Gun Street girl again.

Never kiss a Gun Street girl again,

I'll never kiss a Gun Street girl again.

Chorus 3   As Chorus 1

Outro | **D5** | **D5** | **D5** | **D5**   ‖

84

House Where Nobody Lives

Words & Music by Tom Waits

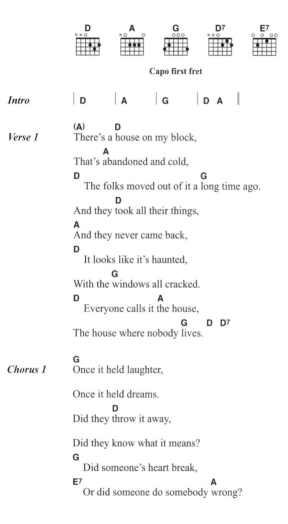

Capo first fret

Intro | D | A | G | D A ‖

Verse 1
     (A)   **D**
There's a house on my block,
            A
That's abandoned and cold,
D   **G**
    The folks moved out of it a long time ago.
            D
And they took all their things,
A
And they never came back,
D
    It looks like it's haunted,
         G
With the windows all cracked.
D   **A**
    Everyone calls it the house,
                    G   **D** **D7**
The house where nobody lives.

Chorus 1
G
Once it held laughter,

Once it held dreams.
          D
Did they throw it away,

Did they know what it means?
G
    Did someone's heart break,
E7   **A**
    Or did someone do somebody wrong?

Verse 2

(A)   **D**
Well, the paint was all cracked,

A
It was peeled off of the wood.

D   **G**
  The papers were stacked on   the porch where I stood.

D
  And the weeds had grown up,

      A
Just as high as the door.

D
  There were birds in the chimney,

    G
And an old chest of drawers.

         D   **A**
Looks like no one will ever come back,

               G   **D** **D7**
To the house were nobody lives.

Chorus 2

(D7)   **G**
Oh well, once it held laughter,

Once it held dreams.

    D
Did they throw it away,

Did they know what it means?

G
  Did someone's heart break,

E7   **A**
  Or did someone do somebody wrong?

Verse 4

(A)　D
So if you find someone,

　　A
Some - one to have, someone to hold,

　D
Don't trade it for silver,

　　G
Oh, don't trade it for gold.

　　　D
'Cause I have all of life's treasures,

　　　A
And they are fine and they are good.

D
They remind me that houses,

　G
Are just made of wood.

　　　D
What makes a house grand,

　　　A
Oh, it ain't the roof or the doors,

　D
If there's love in a house,

　G
It's a palace for sure.

　　D
Without　love,

　　　A
It ain't nothing but a house,

　　　G　　D
A house where nobody lives.

　　　　　A
Without love it ain't nothing but a house,

　　G　　　D
A house where nobo - dy lives.

How's It Gonna End

Words & Music by Tom Waits & Kathleen Brennan

Am	Am7/G	Dm	E	E/G#

Intro | Am | Am | Am | Am   ‖

Verse 1

Am   Am7/G   Dm
He had three whole dollars, a worn-out car,

      Am   E   Am
And a wife who was leaving for good.

                Am7/G   Dm
Life's made of trouble, worry, pain and struggle,

                                   E7
She wrote 'good-bye' in the dust on the hood.

               Dm
They found a a map of Missouri,

Am
Lipstick on the glass,

        Dm   E7
They must of left in the middle of the night.

Chorus 1

        Dm   E/G#   Am
And I   want to know the same thing,

                  Dm
Everyone wants to know,

        E   Am
How's it gonna end?

Verse 2

Am   **Am7/G**
Behind a smoke-coloured curtain,

Dm
The girl disappeared,

  Am   **E**   **Am**
They found out that the ring was a fake.

      Am7/G
A tree born crooked,

  Dm
Will never grow straight,

                 E7
She sunk like a hammer into the lake.

Dm   **Am**
  A long lost letter and an old leaky boat,

Dm   **E7**
Promises are never meant to keep.

Chorus 2

  Dm **E/G#**   **Am**
And I   want to know the same thing,

I want to know,

Dm   **E**   **Am**
How's it gonna end?

Verse 3

Am   **Am7/G**
The barn leaned over,

  Dm
The vultures dried their wings,

  Am   **E**   **Am**
The moon climbed up an empty sky.

        Am7/G   **Dm**
The sun sank down behind the tree on the hill,

                         E7
There's a killer and he's coming through the rye.

  Dm   **Am**
But maybe he's the father of that lost little girl,

Dm   **E7**
  It's hard to tell in this light.

Chorus 3   As Chorus 1

Bridge 1

Dm
Drag your wagon and your plow,

Over the bones of the dead,

              Am
Out among the roses and the weeds.

Dm
You can never go back,

And the answer is no,

         E7
And wishing for it only makes it bleed.

Verse 4

Am   Am7/G   Dm
Joel Torna - bene was broken on the wheel,

Am   E   Am
Shane and Bum Ma - honey on the lamb.

        Am7/G Dm
The grain was as gold as Sheila's hair,

All the way from Liverpool,

   E7
With all we could steal.

    Dm
He was robbed of twenty dollars,

  Am
His body found stripped,

Dm   E7
Cast into the harbour there and drowned.

Chorus 4

    Dm E/G♯   Am
And I   want to know the same thing,

We all want to know,

Dm   E   Am
How's it gonna end?

                         Am   Am7/G   Dm
Verse 5   The sirens are snaking their way up the hill,
                           Am   E   Am
                 It's last call somewhere in the world.
                              Am7/G
                 The reptiles blend in,
                             Dm
                 With the colour of the street,
                                                    E7
                 Life is sweet at the edge of a razor.
                         Dm   Am
                 And down in the first row of an old picture show,
                         Dm   E7
                 The old man is asleep, the credits start to roll.

Chorus 5   As Chorus 4

Chorus 6   As Chorus 4

                         Dm   E/G♯   Am
Chorus 7   And I   just want to know the same thing,

                 I want to know,
                 Dm   E   Am
                    How's it gonna end?

Outro | Am | Am | Am | Am   ‖

I Hope That I Don't Fall In Love With You

Words & Music by Tom Waits

C   F   G13   G9   G   C/E   Am7   G/B

Intro   ‖: C F | G13 G9 | G9 :‖

Verse 1
              C   F   G13   G9
Well I hope that I don't fall in love with you,
            C   F   G13   G9
'Cause falling in love just makes me blue.
               F   C
Well the music plays and you display,
           G   C
Your heart for me to see,
        F   C/E   F   G13   G9
I had a beer and now I hear you calling out for me.
            C   F   G   C   G13 C G Am7
And I hope that I don't fall in love with you.

Verse 2
           G/B   C   F   G13   G9 Am7
Well the room is crowded, people every - where,
           G/B   C   F   G13   G9
And I wonder, should I offer you a chair?
             F   C
Well if you sit down with this old clown,
         G   C
Take that frown and break it,
           F   C/E
Be - fore the evening's gone away,
        F   G13   G9
I think that we could make it.
            C   F   G   C   G13 C G Am7
And I hope that I don't fall in love with you.

Verse 3

G/B   C   F   G13   G9 G Am7
Well the night does funny things inside a man,

G/B   C   F   G13   G9
These old tom-cat feelings you don't under - stand.

      F   C
Well I turn around to look at you,

       G   C
You light a ciga - rette.

  F   C/E
I wish I had the guts to bum one,

F   G13   G9
But we've never met.

Am7 G/B C   F   G   C   G13 C G Am7
And I   hope that I don't fall in love with you.

Verse 4

G/B C   F   G13   G9 G Am7
I can see that you are lonesome just like me,

G/B C   F   G13 G9
And it being late, you'd like some compa - ny.

      F   C
Well I turn around to look at you,

       G   C
And you look back at me.

      F   C/E
The guy you're with he's up and split,

       F   G13   G9
The chair next to you's free.

Am7 G/B C   F   G   C   G13 C G
And I   hope that you don't fall in love with me.

Verse 5

G/B   C   F   G13   G9
Now it's closing time, the music's fading out,

      C   F   G13   G9
Last call for drinks, I'll have another stout.

      F   C
Well I turn around to look at you,

G   C
  You're nowhere to be found.

  F   C/E
I search the place for your lost face,

       F   G13   G9
Guess I'll have another round.

Am7 G/B C   F   G9   C   G13 C G C
And I   think that I just fell in love with you.

I Never Talk To Strangers

Words & Music by Tom Waits

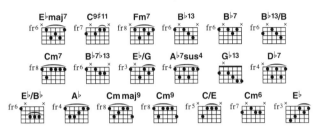

Intro

Eᵇmaj7 C9♯11   Fm7 Bᵇ13 Bᵇ7

Bartender I'd like a Manhattan please.

| Eᵇmaj7 C9♯11 | Fm7 Bᵇ13 Bᵇ7 ‖

Verse 1

Eᵇmaj7   C9♯11
  Stop me if you've heard this one,

Fm7   Bᵇ13   Bᵇ7
  I feel as though we've met before.

Eᵇmaj7 C9♯11
  Per - haps I am mistaken.

Fm7   Bᵇ13   Bᵇ13/B
  But it's just that I re - mind you of,

      Cm7   Fm7
Some - one you used to care about,

                                        Bᵇ7   Bᵇ7ᵇ13
Oh but that was long a - go.

Eᵇmaj7
  Now tell me do you really think,

      C9♯11
I'd fall for that old line,

  Fm7   Bᵇ13   Bᵇ7
I was not born just yester - day.

      Eᵇmaj7 Eᵇ/G Aᵇ7sus4 Cm7   Gᵇ13   Fm7 Bᵇ7
Besides I never   talk to strangers any - way.

Verse 2

  (Bᵇ7)   Eᵇmaj7   C9♯11
Well I ain't a bad guy when you get to know me,

Fm7   Bᵇ13
  I just thought there ain't no harm.

Bᵇ7   Eᵇmaj7   C9♯11
Hey just try minding your own business bud,

cont.

Fm7   Bb13
Who asked you to an - noy me,

Bb13/B Cm7   Db7
 With your sad, sad repar - tee?

     Eb/Bb   Ab7sus4 Db7   Gb13 Fm7 Bb7
Besides I never talk to strangers any - way.

Bridge

    Ab   Db7
Your life's a dimestore novel,

Eb/Bb   Bb7   Ebmaj7
 This town is full of guys like you.

     Ab   Db7
And you're looking for some - one,

 Eb/Bb Bb7   Ebmaj7
To take the place of her.

   Bb13/B   Cm7
You might be reading my mail.

     Cm maj9
And you're bitter 'cause he left you,

      Cm7   Cm9
That's why you're drinking in this bar,

    Ab   C/E
Well, only suckers fall in love,

     Fm7   Bb7b13
With perfect strang - ers.

Verse 3

(Bb7b13) Ebmaj7 C9#11
It always takes one   to know one, stranger,

Fm7   Bb13
 Maybe we're just wiser now.

Bb7 Ebmaj7   C9#11   Fm7
Yeah, and been around the block so many times,

     Bb13
That we don't notice.

Bb13/B Cm7
That we're all just perfect strangers,

   Cm maj9
As long as we ignore,

    Cm7
That we all begin as strangers,

Cm6
Just before we find,

   Eb/Bb   Bb7sus4 Bb7 Ebmaj7 Db7 Gb13
We really aren't strangers any - more.

Eb
Oh you don't look like such a chump.

Oh baby.

I Wish I Was In New Orleans

Words & Music by Tom Waits

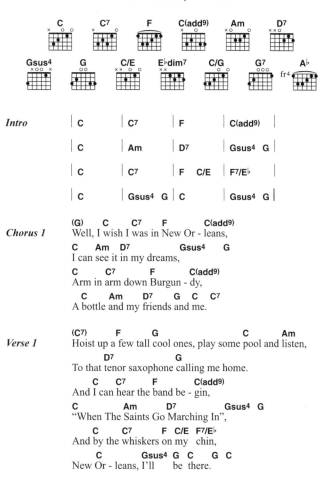

Intro

C	C7	F	C(add9)
C	Am	D7	Gsus4 G
C	C7	F C/E	F7/Eb
C	Gsus4 G	C	Gsus4 G

Chorus 1

(G)   C   C7   F   C(add9)
Well, I wish I was in New Or - leans,

C Am D7   Gsus4   G
I can see it in my dreams,

C   C7   F   C(add9)
Arm in arm down Burgun - dy,

   C   Am   D7   G C C7
A bottle and my friends and me.

Verse 1

(C7)   F   G   C   Am
Hoist up a few tall cool ones, play some pool and listen,

        D7   G
To that tenor saxophone calling me home.

     C   C7   F   C(add9)
And I can hear the band be - gin,

C   Am   D7   Gsus4 G
"When The Saints Go Marching In",

     C   C7   F C/E F7/Eb
And by the whiskers on my chin,

      C   Gsus4 G C   G C
New Or - leans, I'll   be there.

Verse 2

(C)   F   G   C   Am
I'll drink you under the table, be red-nosed, go for walks,

     D7   G
The old haunts what I wants is red beans and rice.

      C   C7   F   C(add9)
And wear the dress I like so well,

      C   Am   D7   Gsus4 G
And meet me at the old saloon,

C   C7   F   C/E F7/E♭
Make sure there's a Dix - ie   moon,

     C   Gsus4 G C   G C
New Orleans, I'll   be there.

Verse 3

(C)   F   G   C   Am
And deal the cards roll the dice, if it ain't that old Chuck E. Weiss,

           D7   G
And Claiborne Avenue, me and you, Sam Jones and all.

Chorus 2

(G)   C   C7   F   C(add9)
And I wish I was in New Or - leans,

        C   Am D7   Gsus4 G
'Cause I can see it in my dreams,

C   C7   F   C/E F7/E♭
Arm in arm down Bur- gun - dy,

  C/G G7   C/G   G7
A bottle and my friends and me,

     C/G   D7 G7 A♭   C
New Orleans, I'll be there.

I Don't Wanna Grow Up

Words & Music by Tom Waits & Kathleen Brennan

D   Asus4   Bm   F♯m   G

Intro | D | D | Asus4 | D ||

Verse 1

D
When I'm lying in my bed at night,
Asus4   D
I don't wanna grow up.

Nothing ever seems to turn out right,
Asus4   D
I don't wanna grow up.
Bm   F♯m
How do you move in a world of fog,
        G   Asus4
That's always chang - ing things?
Bm   F♯m   G   Asus4
Makes me wish that I could be a dog.

Verse 2

D
Oh well, when I see the price that you pay,
Asus4   D
I don't wanna grow up.

I don't ever wanna be that way,
Asus4   D
I don't wanna grow up.
Bm   F♯m
Seems like folks turn into things
         G   Asus4
That they'd never want,
   Bm   F♯m   G   Asus4
The only thing to live for is to - day.

Verse 3

        D
I'm gonna put a hole in my T.V. set,

Asus⁴   **D**
I don't wanna grow up.

Open up the medicine chest,

     Asus⁴   **D**
And I don't wanna grow up.

Bm   **F♯m**
I don't wanna have to shout it out,

Bm   **F♯m**
I don't want my hair to fall out,

Bm   **F♯m**
I don't wanna be filled with doubt,

Bm   **F♯m**
I don't wanna be a good boy scout,

Bm   **F♯m**
I don't wanna have to learn to count,

Bm   **F♯m**
I don't wanna have the biggest amount,

G   **Asus⁴**   **D**
And I don't wanna grow up.

Verse 4

D
Well when I see my parents fight,

Asus⁴   **D**
I don't wanna grow up.

They all go out and drinking all night,

     Asus⁴   **D**
And I don't wanna grow up.

     Bm   **F♯m**
I'd rather stay here in my room,

Bm   **F♯m**
Nothing out there but sad and gloom.

Bm   **F♯m**   **G**   **Asus⁴**
I don't wanna live in a big old tomb on Grand Street.

Verse 5

D
When I see the 5 o'clock news,

Asus⁴   **D**
I don't wanna grow up.

They comb their hair and shine their shoes.

Asus⁴   **D**
I don't wanna grow up.

Bm   **F♯m**
Stay around in my old hometown,

Bm   **F♯m**
I don't wanna put no money down,

Bm   **F♯m**
I don't wanna get me a big old loan,

Bm   **F♯m**
Work them fingers to the bone.

Bm   **F♯m**
I don't wanna float a broom,

Bm   **F♯m**
Fall in love and get married then boom,

Bm   **F♯m**
How the hell did I get here so soon?

G   **Asus⁴**   **D**
I don't wanna grow up.

In The Neighborhood

Words & Music by Tom Waits

D   G   Bm   Em   Asus⁴   A   D/F♯   D/A

Capo first fret

Verse 1

          D   **G**
Well, the eggs chase the bacon,

        D   **G**
Round the frying pan,

          D   **Bm**
And the whining dog pidgeons,

          Em   **Asus⁴** **A**
By the steeple bell rope.

         D   **G**
And the dogs tipped the garbage pails,

D   **G**
Over last night,

          D   **Bm**
And there's always con - struction work,

Em   **A**
Bothering you.

       D/F♯   **G**
In the neighbor - hood.

       D/F♯   **G**
In the neighbor - hood.

      D/A   **A**   **D**
In the neigh - bor - hood.

Verse 2

      D   **G**
Well Friday's a fune - ral,

      D   **G**
And Saturday's a bride,

D   **Bm**   **Em**   **Asus⁴**
Sey's got a pistol on the register side.

A   **D**   **G**
And the goddam de - livery trucks,

D   **G**
They make too much noise.

       D   **Bm**
And we don't get our butter,

    Em   **A**
De - livered no more.

    D/F♯   **G**
In the neighbor - hood.

    D/F♯   **G**
In the neighbor - hood.

    D/A   **A**   **D**
In the neigh - bor - hood.

Verse 3

      D   **G**
Well Big Mambo's kicking,

     D   **G**
His old grey - hound,

      D   **Bm**
And the kids can't get ice cream,

       Em   **Asus⁴**
'Cause the market burned down.

A   **D**   **G**
And the newspaper sleeping bags,

D   **G**
Blow down the lane,

       D   **Bm**
And that goddam flatbed's

    Em   **A**
Got me pinned in a - gain.

    D/F♯   **G**
In the neighbor - hood.

    D/F♯   **G**
In the neighbor - hood.

    D/A   **A**   **D**
In the neigh - bor - hood.

```
                 D          G
There's a couple of Filipino girls,
D                  G
Giggling by the church.
              D        Bm
And the window is busted,
            Em              Asus4    A
And the landlord ain't home.
              D          G
And Butch joined the army,
              D          G
Yeah, that's where he's been.
              D          Bm
And the jackhammer's digging,
              Em              A
Up the sidewalks a - gain.
            D/F♯       G
In the neighbor - hood.
            D/F♯       G
In the neighbor - hood.
             D/A    A    D
In the neigh - bor - hood.
            D/F♯       G
In the neighbor - hood.
            D/F♯       G
In the neighbor - hood.
             D/A    A    D
In the neigh - bor - hood.
```

Innocent When You Dream (78)

Words & Music by Tom Waits

Intro

| F | F | F | F |

| F | F | F |

Verse 1

    F   F#dim7 Gm
The bats are in the   belfry,

      C7   F
The dew is on the moor,

         A7   Dm
Where are the arms that held me,

    B♭   F
And pledged her love be - fore,

    B♭   C7   F
And pledged her love be - fore?

Chorus 1

F   F#dim7 Gm
It's such a sad old feeling,

    C7   F
The hills are soft and green.

          F7   B♭   Gm
It's memories that I'm stealing,

         F   B♭   C
But you're innocent when you dream,

B♭   C
When you dream,

      F   B♭   C
You're innocent when you dream,

B♭   C
When you dream,

      F   B♭   F
You're innocent when you dream.

Link 1 | F | F | F | F   ‖

Verse 2
F   F♯dim7 Gm
I made a golden promise,
C7   F
     That we would never part,
   A7   Dm
I gave my love a locket,
      B♭   F
And then I broke her heart,
      B♭   C7   F
And then I broke her heart.

Chorus 2
F   F♯dim7 Gm
It's such a sad old feeling,
        C7   F
The fields are soft and green.
                F7   B♭   Gm
It's memories that I'm stealing,
             F   B♭   C
But you're innocent when you dream,
B♭   C
When you dream,
          F   B♭   C
You're innocent when you dream,
F   B♭   F
Innocent when you dream.

Verse 3
F   F♯dim7   Gm
Running through the graveyard,
       C7   F
We laughed my friends and I.
       A7   Dm
We swore we'd be to - gether,
        B♭   F
Un - til the day we died,
        B♭   C7   F
Un - til the day we died.

Chorus 3

F   F#dim7 Gm
And it's such a sad old feeling,

   C7   F
The fields are soft and green.

              F7   Bb   Gm
It's memories that I'm stealing,

              F   Bb   C
But you're innocent when you dream,

Bb   C
When you dream,

            F   Bb   C
You're innocent when you dream,

Bb   F
When you dream.

Invitation To The Blues

Words & Music by Tom Waits

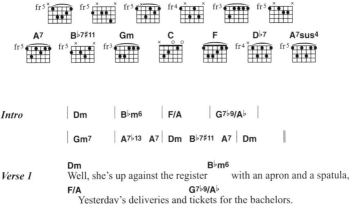

Intro | Dm | B♭m6 | F/A | G7♭9/A♭ |

| Gm7 | A7♭13 A7 | Dm B♭7♯11 A7 | Dm   ‖

Verse 1

Dm
Well, she's up against the register   B♭m6
with an apron and a spatula,

F/A
   Yesterday's deliveries and tickets for the bachelors.   G7♭9/A♭

     Gm7   A7♭13   A7
She's a moving violation from her conk down to her shoes,

          Dm   B♭7♯11 A7   Dm
Well, it's just an invi - tation   to the blues.

Verse 2

(Dm)   Gm   C
And you feel just like Cagney, she looks like Rita Hayworth,

        F
At the counter of the Schwab's drugstore.

        Gm   C
You wonder if she might be single, she's a loner and likes to mingle,

F   A7
Got to be patient, try and pick up a clue.

Verse 3

  (A7)   **Dm**   **B♭m6**

She said, "How you gonna like 'em, over medium or scrambled?",

F/A   **G7♭9/A♭**   **D♭7**

You say "Anyway's the only way", be careful not to gamble,

      Gm7   **A7♭13**   **A7**

On a guy with a suitcase and a ticket getting out of here.

      Dm   **B♭m6**

In a tired bus station in an old pair of shoes,

      A7sus4   **A7**   **Dm**

This ain't nothing but an invi - tation to the blues.

Verse 4

(Dm)   **Gm**   **C**

But you can't take your eyes off her, get an - other cup of java,

      F

It's just the way she pours it for you, joking with the customers.

      Gm   **C**

Mercy mercy, Mr. Percy, there ain't nothing back in Jersey,

      F   **A7**

But a broken-down jalopy of a man I left behind.

      Dm   **B♭m6**

And the dream that I was chasing, and a battle with booze,

      A7   **Dm**

And an open invitation to the blues.

Verse 5

(Dm)   **Gm**   **C**

But she used to have a sugar daddy and a candy-apple Caddy,

      F

And a bank account and everything, accustomed to the finer things.

      Gm

He probably left her for a socialite,

      C

And he didn't love her 'cept at night,

      F   **A7**

And then he's drunk and never even told her that he cared.

      Dm   **B♭m6**

So they took the registration, and the car-keys and her shoes,

      A7♭13   **A7**   **(Dm)**

And left her with an invi - tation to the blues.

Sax. solo | **Dm** | **B♭m6** | **F/A** | **G7♭9/A♭** |

                    | **Gm7** | **A7♭13 A7** | **Dm B♭7♯11 A7** | **Dm** ‖

Verse 6

(Dm)   Gm
'Cause there's a Continental Trailways,

      C
Leaving local bus tonight, good evening,

F
   You can have my seat, I'm sticking 'round here for a while.

      Gm   C
Get me a room at the Squire, the filling station's hiring,

   F   A7
And I can eat here every night, what the hell have I got to lose?

      Dm   B♭m6
Got a crazy sensation, go or stay? Now I gotta choose,

          A7♭13   A7   (Dm)
And I'll ac - cept your invi - tation to the blues.

Outro | Dm | B♭m6 | F/A | G7♭9/A♭ |

              | Gm7 | A7♭13 A7 | Dm B♭7♯11 A7 | Dm   ‖

Jersey Girl

Words & Music by Tom Waits

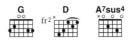

Intro

‖: G | G | D | D |
| A7sus4 | A7sus4 | D | D :‖

Verse 1

(D)   **G**
Got no time for the corner boys,

                    D
Down in the street making all that noise.

                           A7sus4
Don't want no whores on Eighth Avenue,

                    D
'Cause tonight I'm gonna be with you.

Verse 2

D   **G**
'Cause tonight I'm gonna take that ride,

                D
Across the river to the Jersey side.

                    A7sus4
Take my baby to the carnival,

                D
And I'll take you all on the rides.

Verse 3

D   **G**
Down the shore every - thing's alright,

                  D
You with your baby on a Saturday night.

                    A7sus4
Don't you know all my dreams come true,

                    D
When I'm walking down the street with you.

Chorus 1

D   G
Sing, sha la, la, la, la.

              D
Sha la, la, la, la, la, la, la.

              A7sus4
Sha la, la, sha la, la, la.

              D
Sha la, la, la, I'm in love with a Jersey girl.

              G
Sha la, la, la, la, la, la.

              D
Sha la, la, la, la, la, la, la, la, la.

              A7sus4
Sha la, la, sha la, la, la.

              D
Sha la, la, la, la, la.

Verse 4

D   G
You know she thrills me with all her charms,

                        D
When I'm wrapped up in my baby's arms.

              A7sus4
My little angel gives me everything,

                D
I know someday that she'll wear my ring.

Verse 5

D   G
So don't bother me 'cause I got no time,

                    D
I'm on my way to see that girl of mine.

                    A7sus4
Nothing else matters in this whole wide world,

                D
When you're in love with a Jersey girl.

Chorus 2   As Chorus 1

Bridge

D   A7sus4   D
And I call your   name,

              A7sus4   D
I can't sleep at   night.

Chorus 3   As Chorus 1   *Repeat to fade*

Jesus Gonna Be Here

Words & Music by Tom Waits

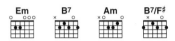

Intro

‖: Em | Em | Em | Em :‖

With vocal ad lib.

Verse 1

N.C.   **Em**
Well, Jesus gonna be here,

He gonna be here soon, yeah.

He's gonna cover us up with leaves,
       B7
With a blanket from the moon, yeah.
  Em
With a promise and a vow,
   Am
And a lullaby for my brow.
      Em
Well, Jesus gonna be here,
B7/F♯   **Em**
 He gonna be here soon, yeah.

Verse 2

N.C.   **Em**
Well, I'm not gonna do nothing but wait here,

I don't have to shout,

I got me no reason, yeah,
   B7
And I got no doubt, yeah.
  Em
I'm gonna get myself unfurled,
   Am
From this mortal coiled up world.

cont.

       Em
Jesus gonna be here,

B7/F♯   **Em**
  Gonna be here soon, yeah.

Verse 3

N.C.   **Em**
I got to keep my eyes, a-keep 'em wide open, yeah,

So I can see my Lord, yeah.

I'm gonna watch the horizon,

              B7
For my brand new Ford, yeah.

            Em
Well, I can hear him rolling on down the lane,

     Am
I said Hollywood be thy name.

           Em
'Cause Jesus gonna be here,

B7/F♯   **Em**
  He's gonna be here soon, yeah.

Verse 4

N.C.   **Em**
Well I've got to keep myself, keep myself faithful,

And you know I've been so good, yeah.

Except for drinking,

              B7
But he knew that I would, yeah.

            Em
And when I'm gonna leave this place better,

        Am
Than the way I found that it was.

           Em
And Jesus gonna be here,

B7/F♯   **B7**
  Gonna be here soon.

N.C.   **Em**
I know my Jesus gonna be here,

        B7/F♯ **Em**
He gonna be here soon, yeah.

N.C.   **Em**
I know my Jesus gonna be here,

B7/F♯   **Em**
  Gonna be here soon, yeah.

Jockey Full Of Bourbon

Words & Music by Tom Waits

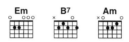

Intro ‖: Em | B7 | B7 | Em :‖

Verse 1

Em
Edna Million in a drop-dead suit,

B7
Dutch Pink on a downtown train.

Two-dollar pistol but the gun won't shoot,

Em
I'm in the corner on the pouring rain.

Sixteen men on a dead man's chest,

B7
And I've been drinking from a broken cup.

Two pairs of pants and a mohair vest,

Em
I'm full of bourbon, I can't stand up.

Chorus 1

Am   Em
Hey little bird, fly away home,

B7   Em
Your house is on fire, children are alone.

Am   Em
Hey little bird, fly away home,

B7   Em
Your house is on fire, your children are alone.

Verse 2

Em
Schiffer broke a bottle on Morgan's head,

B7
And I'm stepping on the devil's tail.

cont.   Across the stripes of a full moon's head,

                              Em
           And through the bars of a Cuban jail.

           Bloody fingers on a purple knife,

                            B7
           Flamingo drinking from a cocktail glass.

           I'm on the lawn with someone else's wife,

                              Em
           Admire the view from up on top of the mast.

Chorus 2   As Chorus 1

Guitar solo   ‖: **Em** | **Em** | **Em** | **B7** |

                 | **B7** | **B7** | **B7** | **Em**   :‖

Chorus 3   As Chorus 1

                 Em
Verse 3   Yellow sheets on a Hong Kong bed,

                          B7
           Stazybo horn and a Slingerland ride.

           "To the carnival," is what she said,

                            Em
           A hundred dollars makes it dark inside.

           Edna Million in a drop-dead suit,

                    B7
           Dutch Pink on a downtown train.

           Two-dollar pistol but the gun won't shoot,

                       Em
           I'm in the corner on the pouring rain.

Chorus 4   As Chorus 1

Guitar solo   ‖: **Em** | **Em** | **Em** | **B7** |

                 | **B7** | **B7** | **B7** | **Em**   :‖   *To fade*

Just The Right Bullets

Words & Music by Tom Waits

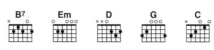

Capo first fret

Verse 1

           B7   **Em**
There is a light in the forest,

           D   **G**
There is a face in the tree.

         B7   **Em**
I'll pull you out of the chorus,

          C   **B7**   **Em**
And the first one's always free.

          C   **D**   **Em**
You can never go a-hunt - ing,

            C   **D**   **Em**
With just a flintlock and a hound.

          B7   **Em**
You won't go home with a bunting,

       C **B7**   **Em**
If you blow a hundred rounds.

Verse 2

           B7   **Em**
It takes much more than wild courage,

         D   **G**
Or you'll hit the tattered clouds.

        B7   **Em**
You must have just the right bullets,

         C   **B7** **Em**
And the first one's always free.

           C   **D**   **Em**
You must be careful in the forest,

        C   **D** **Em**
Broken glass and rusty nails.

         B7   **Em**
If you're to bring back something for us,

        C **B7** **Em**
I have bullets   for sale.

Interlude
faster

| Em | Em | Em | Em ‖

‖: Em | Em | D | D :‖

| B7 | B7 | B7 | B7 | Em ‖

Verse 3
a tempo

　　　　　　　B7　　　　　　Em
Why be a fool when you can chase away,

　　　D　　　　　　　　　　G
Your blind and your gloom?

　　　　　　　B7　　　　　　　　　　　　Em
But I have blessed each one of these bullets,

　　　　　　C　　　B7　Em
And they shine just like a spoon.

　　　　　C　　D　　Em
To have sixty silver wishes,

　　　C　　D　　Em
Is a small price to pay,

　　　　　　　B7　　　　　　　　　Em
They'll be your private little fishes,

　　　　　　C　　B7　　　Em
And they'll never swim away.

Verse 4

　　　　　B7　　　　Em
I just want you to be happy,

　　　　D　　　　G
That's my only little wish.

　　　　　B7　　　　　　　　Em
I'll fix your wagon and your mus - ket,

　　　　C　　　　　B7　Em
And the spoon will have its dish.

　　　C　　　D　　Em
And I shudder at the thought,

　　　　C　　D　　Em
Of your poor empty hunter's pouch,

　　　　　B7　　　　　Em
So I'll keep the wind from your barrel,

　　　　C　　B7　　Em
And bless the roof of your house.

Outro
faster

Em	Em	Em	Em ‖
‖: Em	Em	D	D
Em	Em	D	D
B7	B7	B7	B7 :‖ Em ‖

Johnsburg, Illinois

Words & Music by Tom Waits

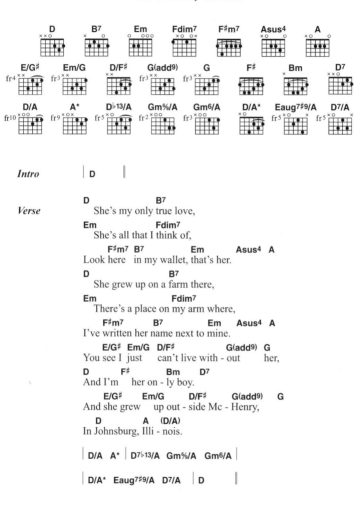

Intro | D   ‖

Verse
D   B7
   She's my only true love,

Em   Fdim7
  She's all that I think of,

    F♯m7 B7   Em   Asus4 A
Look here   in my wallet, that's her.

D   B7
   She grew up on a farm there,

Em   Fdim7
  There's a place on my arm where,

   F♯m7   B7   Em   Asus4 A
I've written her name next to mine.

   E/G♯ Em/G D/F♯   G(add9) G
You see I just   can't live with - out   her,

D   F♯   Bm   D7
And I'm   her on - ly boy.

   E/G♯ Em/G D/F♯   G(add9)   G
And she grew   up out - side Mc - Henry,

   D   A   (D/A)
In Johnsburg, Illi - nois.

| D/A A* | D7♭13/A Gm%/A Gm6/A |

| D/A* Eaug7♯9/A D7/A | D   ‖

Long Way Home

Words & Music by Tom Waits & Kathleen Brennan

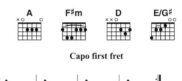

Capo first fret

Intro ‖: A | A | A | A :‖

Verse 1

A
Well I stumbled in the darkness,

I'm lost and alone.

Though I said I'd go before us,
                           F♯m
And show the way back home.
      D   A
Is there a light up a - head?
                      D
I can't hold onto her arm.
        A
For - give me pretty baby,
      E/G♯   A
But I always take the long way home.

Verse 2

A
Money's just something you throw,

Off the back of a train.

Got a head full of lightning,
      F♯m
A hat full of rain.
      D   A
And I know that I said,
               D
I'd never do it a - gain,
          A
And I love you pretty baby,
      E/G♯   A
But I always take the long way home.

Verse 3
       A
I put food on the table,

And a roof overhead.

But I'd trade it all tomorrow,
           F♯m
For the highway in - stead.
         D   **E/G♯**
Watch your back if I should tell you,
  A   **D**
Your love's the only thing I've ever known.
           A
One thing for sure pretty baby,
  E/G♯   **A**
I always take the long way home.

Bridge
E/G♯   **A**
Mmm, mmm,
D   **E/G♯**
Mmm, mmm.

Verse 4
E/G♯   **A**
You know I love you baby,

More than the whole wide world.

You are my woman,
           F♯m
I know you are my pearl.
       D   **E/G♯**
Let's go out past the party lights,
     A   **D**
Where we can finally be a - lone.
      A
Come with me,
    E/G♯   **A**
And we can take the long way home.
  D   **A**
Mmm, come with me,
      E/G♯   **A**
Together we can take the long way home.
  D   **A**
Mmm, come with me,
      E/G♯   **A**   **D** **A** **E/G♯** **A**
Fade   Together we can take the long way home.

(Looking For) The Heart Of Saturday Night

Words & Music by Tom Waits

[Chord diagrams: D, G/B, G/A, G, G/F♯, Em7, A7sus2, D/A, C/G]

Intro

| D | D | G/B G/A | G G/F♯ |

| Em7 | A7sus2 | D/A C/G | D/A C/G ‖

Verse 1

               D/A   C/G   D/A   C/G
Well you gassed her up be - hind the wheel,

                G/B   G/A   G   G/F♯
With your arm around your sweet one in your Oldsmo - bile.

Em7
Barrelling down the boulevard,

A7sus2   D/A   C/G D/A C/G
You're looking for the heart of Saturday night.

Verse 2

               D/A   C/G
And you got paid on Friday,

               D/A   C/G
And your pockets are jingling.

G/B   G/A
And you see the lights,

        G   G/F♯   Em7
You get all tingling cause you're cruising with a six,

A7sus2   D/A   C/G D/A C/G
And you're looking for the heart of Saturday night.

Bridge 1

C/G   G/B
Then you comb your hair,

A7sus2
   Shave your face,

D/A   C/G   D/A   C/G
   Trying to wipe out every trace.

    G/B
Of all the other days,

G   Em7
   In the week you know that this'll be the Saturday,

      A7sus2
You're reaching your peak.

Verse 3

             D/A   C/G
Stopping on the red,

D/A   C/G
   You're going on the green.

       G/B   G/A
   'Cause to - night'll be like nothing

G   G/F♯
You've ever seen.

       Em7
And you're barrelling down the boulevard,

A7sus2   D/A   C/G D/A C/G
   Looking for the heart of Saturday night.

Bridge 2

C/G   G/B   A7sus2
Tell me is it the crack of the poolballs,   neon buzzing?

D/A   C/G   D/A   C/G
   Telephone's ringing; it's your second cousin.

      G/B   G
Is it the barmaid that's smiling   from the corner of her eye?

Em7   A7sus2
Magic of the melancholy tear in your eye.

Verse 4

D/A   C/G   D/A   C/G
Makes it kind of quiver   down in the core,

       G/B   G/A   G   G/F♯
   'Cause you're dreaming of them Saturdays   that came be - fore.

          Em7
And now you're stumbling,

      A7sus2   D/A   C/G D/A C/G
   You're stumbling onto the heart of Saturday night.

Verse 5   As Verse 1

Bridge 3   As Bridge 2

                   D/A   **C/G**   **D/A**   **C/G**
Verse 6   Makes it kind of special   down in the core,
                             G/B   **G/A**   **G**   **G/F♯**
                   And you're dreaming of them Saturdays   that came be - fore.
                             Em7
                   It's found you stumbling,

                   A7sus2   **D/A**   **C/G D/A C/G**
                   Stumbling onto the heart of Saturday night.
                             G/B
                   And you're stumbling,

                   A7sus2   **D/A**   **C/G D/A C/G**
                   Stumbling onto the heart of Saturday night.

                   G/B   **A7sus2 D**
                   Mmm, mmm, mmm.

Lucinda

Words & Music by Tom Waits & Kathleen Brennan

Am	Am7/G	E7	Dm	E7/G#	Dm/F	B7

Capo first fret

Verse 1

              Am
Well they call me William the Pleaser,
                 Am7/G   **E7**
I sold opium, fireworks and lead.
            Am   **Am7/G** **Dm**
Now I'm telling my troubles to strangers,
            Am   **E7**   **Am**
When the shadows get long I'll be dead.

Verse 2

        Am
Now her hair was as black as a bucket of tar,
                       Am7/G   **E7**   **E7/G#**
Her skin was as white as a cuttlefish bone.
        Am   **Am7/G**   **Dm**   **Dm/F**
I left Texas to follow Lu - cinda,
          Am   **E7**   **Am**
Now I'll never see Heaven or home.

Verse 3

        Am
I made a wish on a sliver of moonlight,
                Am7/G   **E7**   **E7/G#**
A sly grin and a bowl full of stars.
        Am   **Am7/G**   **Dm**   **Dm/F**
Like a kid who captures a firefly,
         Am   **E7**   **Am**
And leaves it only to die in the jar.

Verse 4

Am
As I kick at the clouds at my hanging,

          Am7/G E7   E7/G♯
As I swing out over the crowd,

      Am   Am7/G   Dm   Dm/F
I will search every face for Lu - cinda's,

            Am   E7   Am
And she will go off with me down to hell.

Verse 5

Am
I thought I'd broke loose of Lucinda,

              Am7/G   E7   E7/G♯
The rain returned and so did the wind.

        Am   Am7/G   Dm   Dm/F
I cast this burden on the god that's within me,

         Am   E7   Am
And I leave   this old world and go free.

Bridge

    E7   E7/G♯   Am
The devil dances in - side empty pockets,

    E7   E7/G♯   Am
But she didn't want money or pearls.

    Dm   Dm/F   Am
No, that wasn't e - nough for Lucinda,

    B7   E7/G♯
She wasn't that kind of girl.

Verse 6

      Am
Now I've fallen from grace for Lucinda,

              Am7/G   E7   E7/G♯
Whoever thought that hell would be so cold.

        Am   C   Dm   Dm/F
I did well for an old tin can sailor,

       Am   E7   Am
But she wanted the bell in my soul.

Verse 7

Am
I've spoken to God on the mountain,

             Am7/G E7   E7/G♯
And I've swam in the Irish   Sea.

      Am   Am7/G   Dm   Dm/F
I ate fire and drank from the Ganges,

       Am   E7   Am
And I'll beg there for mercy for me.

Harmonica
solo

| Am | | Am | | Am Am⁷/G | E⁷ | |

| Am Am⁷/G | Dm Dm/F | Am E⁷ | Am ‖

Verse 8

Am
I thought I'd broke loose of Lucinda,

                     C   **E⁷**   **E⁷/G♯**
The rain returned and so did the wind.

       Am   **Am⁷/G**   **Dm**   **Dm/F**
I was standing outside the White Horse,

       Am   **E⁷**   **Am**
And then I was a - fraid to go in.

Verse 9

Am
I heard someone pull the trigger,

Her breasts heaved in the moonlight again.

                  Am⁷/G   **Dm**   **Dm/F**
There was a smear of gold in the window,

       Am   **E⁷**   **Am**
And then I was the jewel of her sin.

Verse 10

Am
They call me William the Pleaser,

            Am⁷/G   **E⁷**   **E⁷/G♯**
I sold opium, fireworks and lead.

       Am   **Am⁷/G**   **Dm**   **Dm/F**
Now I'm telling my troubles to strangers,

       Am   **E⁷**   **Am**
When the shadows get long I'll be dead.

Verse 11

Am
Now her hair was as black as a bucket of tar,

                 Am⁷/G   **E⁷**   **E⁷/G♯**
Her skin as white as a cuttlefish bone.

       Am   **Am⁷/G**   **Dm**   **Dm/F**
I left Texas to follow Lu - cinda,

             Am   **E⁷**   **Am**
And I know I'll never see Heaven or home,

        Am   **E⁷**   **Am**
I know I'll never see Heaven or home,

        Am   **E⁷**   **Am**
I know I'll never see Heaven or home.

Make It Rain

Words & Music by Tom Waits & Kathleen Brennan

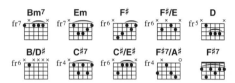

Intro | Bm7 | Bm7 | Bm7 | Bm7 ‖

Verse 1

Bm7
She took all my money and my best friend,

              Em   Bm7
You know the story, here it comes a - gain.

        F#   Em
I have no pride, I have no shame,

              Bm7
You got to make it rain, make it rain.

Verse 2

Bm7
Since you're gone, deep inside it hurts,

    Em   Bm7
I'm just another sad guest on this dark earth.

   F#   Em
I want to believe in the mercy of the world again,

        Bm7
Make it rain, make it rain.

Bridge 1

Em   Bm7
The night's too quiet,   stretched out alone,

F#   F#/E   D   Bm7   B/D#
I need the whip of thun - der and the wind's dark moan.

Em   Bm7
I'm not Abel,   I'm just Cain,

C#7   C#/E#   F#7/A#
Open up the heavens,   make it rain.

Verse 3

                   Bm7
I'm close to Heaven, crushed at the gate,

                   Em   Bm7
They sharpen their knives on my mis - takes.

F#   Em
What she done, you can't give it a name,

          Bm7
You got to   make it rain, make it rain, yeah.

Guitar solo

| Bm7 | Bm7 | Em | Bm7 |

| F# | Em | Bm7 | Bm7 ‖

Bridge 2

Em   Bm7
Without her love,   without your kiss,

F#   F#/E   D   Bm7 B/D#
Hell can't burn me more than this.

Em   Bm7
I'm burning with all this pain,

C#7   C#/E# F#7/A#
Put out the fire,   make it rain.

Verse 4

                   Bm7
I'm born to trouble, I'm born to fate,

         Em   Bm7
In - side a promise I can't escape.

F#   Em
It's the same old world,   but nothing looks the same,

Bm7
Make it rain, make it rain.

F#7   Bm7
   Got to make it rain,

F#7   F#7/A# Bm7
   Make it rain.

          F#7   F#7/A# Bm7
You got to make it   rain,

       F#7 F#7/A# Bm7
Got to   make it rain.

You got to.

F#7 F#7/A#   Bm7
      I stand a - lone here.

F#7   F#7/A# Bm7
   I stand a - lone here.

Sing it,

F#7 F#7/A#   Bm7
      Make it rain,

      F#7 F#7/A# Bm7
Make it rain,

      F#7 F#7/A# Bm7
Make it rain.   *To fade*

Martha

Words & Music by Tom Waits

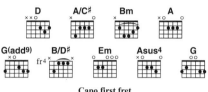

Capo first fret

Intro

‖: D A/C♯ | D A/C♯ | Bm A | G(add9) :‖

Verse 1

  D A/C♯ D   A/C♯
Oper -ator, number, please:

  Bm A G(add9)
It's been so many years,

   D A/C♯ D A/C♯
Will she re - member my old voice,

Bm A   G(add9)
While I fight the tears?

   D B/D♯ Em A
Hel - lo, hel - lo there, is this Martha?

D B/D♯ Em A
This is old Tom Frost.

   D B/D♯ Em   A
And I am calling long distance,

   Bm   A   G(add9)
Don't worry a - bout the cost.

    D   B/D♯ Em   A
'Cause it's been forty years or more,

   D B/D♯ Em A
Now Martha please re - call.

D   B/D♯ Em
Meet me out for coffee,

A   Bm   G(add9)
Where we'll talk about it all.

Chorus 1

       D   **G(add9)**
And those were days of roses,

D   **G(add9)**
Poetry and prose and Martha,

Bm **A**   **G**   **Em Asus4 D**
All I had was you and all you had was   me.

D   **G(add9)**
There was no to - morrows,

      D   **G(add9)**
We'd packed away our sorrows,

      Bm   **A**   **G**   **Asus4 D**
And we saved them for a rain - y   day.

Link 1 | **D A/C♯** | **D A/C♯** | **Bm A** | **G(add9)** ‖

Verse 2

      D   **A/C♯**   **D**   **A/C♯**
And I feel so much older now,

      Bm   **A**   **G(add9)**
And you're much older too,

D   **A/C♯**
How's your husband?

      D   **A/C♯**
And how's your kids?

          Bm A   **G(add9)**
You know that I got married too?

D   **B/D♯**   **Em**   **A**
  Lucky that you found some - one,

    D   **B/D♯**   **Em** **A**
To make you feel se - cure,

       D   **B/D♯ Em**   **A**
'Cause we were all so young and foolish,

Bm   **A**   **G(add9)**
Now we are ma - ture.

Chorus 2   As Chorus 1

Link 2   ‖: **D A/C♯** | **D A/C♯** | **Bm A** | **G(add9)** :‖

Verse 3

       D   **A/C♯**   **D**   **A/C♯**
And I was always so im - pulsive,

    Bm   **A**   **G(add9)**
I guess that I still am,

D   **A/C♯** **D**   **A/C♯**
    And all that really mattered then,

    Bm **A**   **G(add9)**
Was that I was a man.

     D   **B/D♯** **Em**   **A**
I guess that our   being to - gether,

     D   **B/D♯**   **Em**   **A**
Was never meant to be.

     D   **B/D♯** **Em**   **A**
And Martha,   Martha,

    Bm   **A**   **G(add9)**
I love you can't you see?

Chorus 3   As Chorus 1

Link 3   ‖ **D A/C♯** | **D A/C♯** | **Bm A** | **G(add9)** ‖

       D   **A/C♯**   **D**   **A/C♯**
Outro   And I re - member quiet evenings,

  Bm   **A**   **G(add9)**
Trembling close to you.

New Coat Of Paint

Words & Music by Tom Waits

C#m7   F#7   A7   G#7   A7#11

Intro

| C#m7 F#7 | A7 G#7 | C#m7 F#7 | A7 G#7 C#m7 |

| C#m7 F#7 | A7#11 G#7 | C#m7 F#7 | A7#11 G#7 C#m7 |

| C#m7 ‖

Verse 1

C#m7   F#7   A7   G#7
Let's put a new coat of paint on this lonesome old town,
C#m7   F#7   A7   G#7
   Set 'em up, we'll be knocking 'em down.
C#m7   F#7   A7#11   G#7
You wear a dress, baby, and I'll wear a tie,
                      C#m7   F#7   A7   G#7 C#m7
We'll laugh at that old bloodshot moon in that burgun - dy   sky.

Piano solo 1

| C#m7 F#7 | A7 G#7 | C#m7 F#7 | A7 G#7 |

| C#m7 F#7 | A7 G#7 | C#m7 F#7 | A7 G#7 C#m7 |

| C#m7 ‖

Verse 2

C#m7   F#7   A7   G#7
   All our scribbled love dreams are lost or thrown a - way,
C#m7   F#7   A7#11   G#7
   Here amidst the shuffle of an overflowing day.
C#m7   F#7   A7#11   G#7
   Our love needs a trans - fusion so let's shoot it full of wine,
C#m7   F#7   A7   G#7   C#m7
   Fishing for a good time starts with throwing in your line.

Piano solo 2 | C♯m7   F♯7 | A7   G♯7 | C♯m7   F♯7 | A7   G♯7 |

                  | C♯m7   F♯7 | A7   G♯7 | C♯m7   F♯7 | A7 G♯7 C♯m7 |

                  | C♯m7   ‖

Verse 3

           C♯m7   F♯7   A7   G♯7
Let's put a new coat of paint on this lonesome old town,

           C♯m7   F♯7   A7♯11   G♯7
   Set 'em up,   set 'em up, we'll be knocking 'em down.

           C♯m7   F♯7   A7♯11   G♯7
   You wear a dress, baby, I'll wear a tie,

                               C♯m7   F♯7   A7   G♯7   C♯m7
We'll laugh at that old bloodshot moon in that burgundy sky.

Piano solo 3 | C♯m7   F♯7 | A7   G♯7 | C♯m7   F♯7 | A7   G♯7 |

                  | C♯m7   F♯7 | A7   G♯7 | C♯m7   F♯7 | A7 G♯7 C♯m7 ‖

                  ‖: C♯m7   F♯7 | A7   G♯7 C♯m7 :‖ C♯m7   ‖

November

Words & Music by Tom Waits

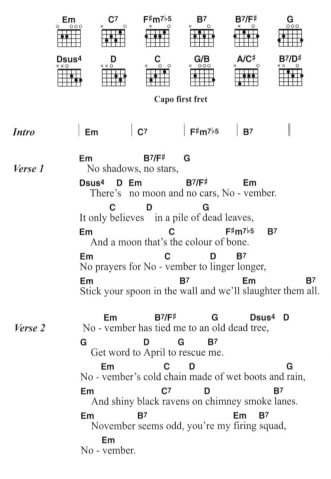

Capo first fret

Intro | Em | C7 | F#m7♭5 | B7 ‖

Verse 1

       Em   **B7/F#**   **G**
    No shadows, no stars,

Dsus4 **D Em**   **B7/F#**   **Em**
    There's   no moon and no cars, No - vember.

          C   **D**   **G**
It only believes   in a pile of dead leaves,

Em   **C**   **F#m7♭5** **B7**
    And a moon that's the colour of bone.

Em   **C**   **D**   **B7**
No prayers for No - vember to linger longer,

Em   **B7**   **Em**   **B7**
Stick your spoon in the wall and we'll slaughter them all.

Verse 2

         Em   **B7/F#**   **G**   **Dsus4** **D**
    No - vember has tied me to an old dead tree,

G   **D**   **G**   **B7**
    Get word to April to rescue me.

       Em   **C**   **D**   **G**
No - vember's cold chain made of wet boots and rain,

Em   **C7**   **D**   **B7**
    And shiny black ravens on chimney smoke lanes.

Em   **B7**   **Em** **B7**
    November seems odd, you're my firing squad,

     Em
No - vember.

| G/B C | A/C♯ D | B7/D♯ Em | B7 | ‖

          Em
Verse 3   With my hair slicked back with carrion shellac,

And the blood from a pheasant and the bone from a hare.

        C   **D**   **G**
Tied to the branches of a roebuck stag,

        Em   **C**   **D**   **B7**
Left to wave in the timber like a buckshot flag.

        Em   **B7**
Go a - way you rainsnout,

Em   **B7**
Go away, blow your brains out,

Em
   November.

Ol' 55

Words & Music by Tom Waits

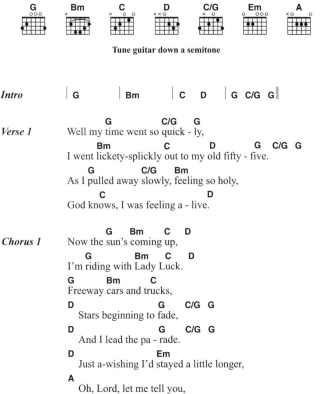

G   Bm   C   D   C/G   Em   A

Tune guitar down a semitone

Intro | G | Bm | C   D | G   C/G   G ‖

Verse 1

         G   C/G   G
Well my time went so quick - ly,

        Bm   C   D   G C/G G
I went lickety-splickly out to my old fifty - five.

       G   C/G   Bm
As I pulled away slowly, feeling so holy,

      C   D
God knows, I was feeling a - live.

Chorus 1

        G   Bm   C   D
Now the sun's coming up,

      G   Bm   C   D
I'm riding with Lady Luck.

G   Bm   C
Freeway cars and trucks,

D   G   C/G G
   Stars beginning to fade,

D   G   C/G G
   And I lead the pa - rade.

D   Em
   Just a-wishing I'd stayed a little longer,

A
   Oh, Lord, let me tell you,

         D
That the feeling's getting stronger.

Verse 2
```
                 G        C/G    G
And it's six in the morn - ing,
Bm                      C      D        G   C/G  G
Gave me no warning, I had to be on my way.
                 G            C/G    G
Well, there's trucks all a - passing me,
                 Bm
And the lights all are flashing,
       C                          D
I'm on my way home from your place.
```

Chorus 2   As Chorus 1

Verse 3
```
                 G            C/G    G
And my time went so quick - ly,
         Bm              C       D        G   C/G  G
I went lickety-splickly out to my old fifty - five.
       G            C/G   G   Bm
As I pulled away slow- ly,  feeling so holy,
       C                     D
God knows, I was feeling a - live.
```

Chorus 3
```
                   G     Bm    C    D
And now the sun's coming up,
       G           Bm   C    D
I'm riding with Lady Luck.
G        Bm        C      D
Freeway cars and trucks,
G        Bm        C      D
Freeway cars and trucks,
G        Bm        C      D   G  C/G  G
Freeway cars and trucks.
```

On A Foggy Night

Words & Music by Tom Waits

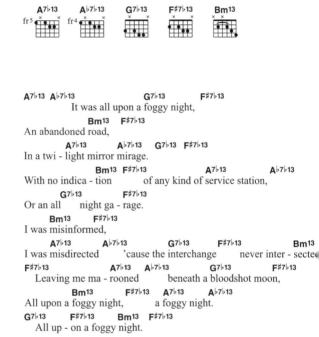

Verse 1

A7♭13 A♭7♭13   G7♭13   F♯7♭13
                It was all upon a foggy night,

                      Bm13   F♯7♭13
An abandoned road,

                A7♭13   A♭7♭13   G7♭13 F♯7♭13
In a twi - light mirror mirage.

                      Bm13 F♯7♭13   A7♭13   A♭7♭13
With no indica - tion   of any kind of service station,

          G7♭13   F♯7♭13
Or an all   night ga - rage.

          Bm13   F♯7♭13
I was misinformed,

          A7♭13   A♭7♭13   G7♭13   F♯7♭13   Bm13
I was misdirected   'cause the interchange   never inter - sected

F♯7♭13   A7♭13   A♭7♭13   G7♭13   F♯7♭13
      Leaving me ma - rooned   beneath a bloodshot moon,

                Bm13   F♯7♭13   A7♭13   A♭7♭13
All upon a foggy night,   a foggy night.

G7♭13   F♯7♭13   Bm13   F♯7♭13
      All up - on a foggy night.

Verse 2

(F♯7♭13)   A7♭13   A♭7♭13
      It was kind of an a - bandoned road,

                G7♭13   F♯7♭13
In a blurred brocade col - lage,

Bm13   F♯7♭13   A7♭13   A♭7♭13
      Is that a road motel?   I can't really tell.

G7♭13   F♯7♭13   Bm13   F♯7♭13
      You got to tell me   is that a vacancy lodge?

      A7♭13   **A♭7♭13**

There's no consolation,

        G7♭13   **F♯7♭13**   **Bm13**   **F♯7♭13**

What kind of situation   to be aimlessly skewed,

A7♭13   **A♭7♭13**

   Amidst a powder blue?

G7♭13 **F♯7♭13**   **Bm13**   **F♯7♭13**

No tell tail light clue.

      A7♭13   **A♭7♭13**   **G7♭13** **F♯7♭13**

And   spun just like the spell you spin,

          Bm13   **F♯7♭13**

This preca - rious pandemo - nium.

A7♭13   **A♭7♭13**   **G7♭13**   **F♯7♭13**   **Bm13**   **F♯7♭13**

   Rosalind, I'm strand - ed, all up - on a foggy night.

Instrumental   ‖: **A7♭13** **A♭7♭13** | **G7♭13** **F♯7♭13** | **Bm13** **F♯7♭13** :‖

Verse 3

  A7♭13   **A♭7♭13**   **G7♭13** **F♯7♭13**   **Bm13** **F♯7♭13**

   Like a sweep - stake ticket for a Broadway ar - cade,

       A7♭13 A♭7♭13   **G7♭13** **F♯7♭13**

Heads you win,   tails I lose.

     Bm13   **F♯7♭13**   **A7♭13**   **A♭7♭13**

And rambling   and gamb - ling,

      G7♭13   **F♯7♭13**   **Bm13**   **F♯7♭13**

All upon a foggy night,   foggy night.

       A7♭13 **A♭7♭13**

Foggy night,

     G7♭13 **F♯7♭13**

Foggy night.

       Bm13   **F♯7♭13**

You've got the vice grips on my personality,

A7♭13 A♭7♭13   **G7♭13** **F♯7♭13**

   It's all upon a foggy night,

        Bm13   **F♯7♭13**

All upon a foggy night.

       A7♭13   **A♭7♭13**

All upon a foggy night.

     G7♭13   **F♯7♭13**

On a foggy night,

All upon a foggy,

        Bm13

All upon a foggy night.

The Piano Has Been Drinking (Not Me)

Words & Music by Tom Waits

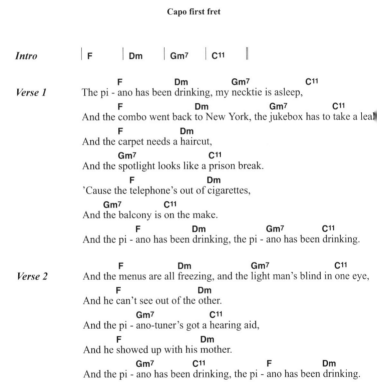

Capo first fret

Intro | F | Dm | Gm⁷ | C¹¹   ‖

Verse 1
```
            F                  Dm            Gm⁷            C¹¹
The pi - ano has been drinking, my necktie is asleep,
            F                  Dm                 Gm⁷            C¹¹
And the combo went back to New York, the jukebox has to take a leak,
            F              Dm
And the carpet needs a haircut,
     Gm⁷                    C¹¹
And the spotlight looks like a prison break.
                F              Dm
'Cause the telephone's out of cigarettes,
     Gm⁷            C¹¹
And the balcony is on the make.
                F              Dm            Gm⁷            C¹¹
And the pi - ano has been drinking, the pi - ano has been drinking.
```

Verse 2
```
            F              Dm            Gm⁷                C¹¹
And the menus are all freezing, and the light man's blind in one eye,
            F              Dm
And he can't see out of the other.
            Gm⁷                C¹¹
And the pi - ano-tuner's got a hearing aid,
            F              Dm
And he showed up with his mother.
            Gm⁷            C¹¹                F            Dm
And the pi - ano has been drinking, the pi - ano has been drinking.
```

      Gm⁷   **C**¹¹   **F**   **Dm**

As the bouncer is a Sumo wrestler cream-puff Caspar Milquetoast.

      Gm⁷   **C**¹¹   **F**   **Dm**

And the owner is a mental midget with the I.Q. of a fence post.

         Gm⁷   **C**¹¹   **F**   **Dm**

'Cause the pi - ano has been drinking, the pi - ano has been drinking.

      Gm⁷   **C**¹¹ **F**   **Dm**

And you can't find your waitress with a Geiger counter,

      Gm⁷   **C**¹¹

And she hates you and your friends,

    F   **Dm**

And you just   can't get served with - out her.

      Gm⁷   **C**¹¹   **F**   **Dm**

And the box-office is drooling, and the bar stools are on fire.

      Gm⁷   **C**¹¹   **F**   **Dm**

And the newspapers were fooling, and the ash-trays have re - tired.

      Gm⁷   **C**¹¹   **F**   **Dm**

'Cause the pi - ano has been drinking, the pi - ano has been drinking,

      Gm⁷   **C**¹¹   **C**⁷

The pi - ano has been drink - ing,

    F   **Dm**   **Gm**⁷   **C**¹¹   **F**

Not me, not me, not me, not me, not me.

Picture In A Frame

Words & Music by Tom Waits & Kathleen Brennan

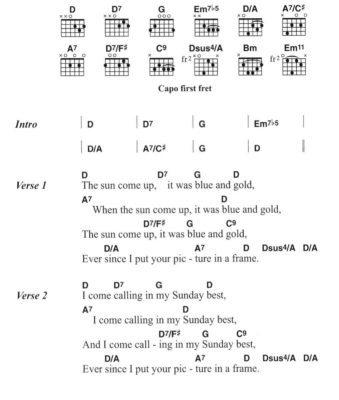

D   D7   G   Em7♭5   D/A   A7/C♯

A7   D7/F♯   C9   Dsus4/A   Bm   Em11

Capo first fret

Intro

| D | D7 | G | Em7♭5 |

| D/A | A7/C♯ | G | D |

Verse 1

D   D7   G   D
The sun come up,   it was blue and gold,

A7   D
   When the sun come up, it was blue and gold,

                          D7/F♯   G   C9
The sun come up, it was blue and gold,

          D/A   A7   D   Dsus4/A   D/A
Ever since I put your pic - ture in a frame.

Verse 2

D   D7   G   D
I come calling in my Sunday best,

A7   D
   I come calling in my Sunday best,

                          D7/F♯   G   C9
And I come call - ing in my Sunday best,

          D/A   A7   D   Dsus4/A   D/A
Ever since I put your pic - ture in a frame.

Bridge

       G   **A7**
And I'm gonna love you,

       D   **Bm**
Till the wheels come off,

Em11 **A7**
Oh,   yeah.

Instrumental

D	**D7**	**G**	**D**	
A7	**A7**	**D**	**D**	
D	**D7/F♯**	**G**	**C9**	
D/A	**A7**	**D Dsus4/A**	**D/A**	

Verse 3

D   **D7**   **G**   **D**
   And I love you baby and I always will,

A7   **D**
  I love you baby and I always will,

         D7/F♯   **G**   **C9**
I love you baby and I always will,

      D/A   **A7**   **D**   **Dsus4/A** **D/A**
Ever since I put your pic - ture in a frame.

         D7/F♯   **G**   **C9**
I love you baby and I always will,

      D/A   **A7**   **D**   **Dsus4/A** **D/A**
Ever since I put your pic - ture in a frame.

      D/A   **A7**   **D**   **Dsus4/A** **D/A**
Ever since I put your pic - ture in a frame.

      D   **A7**   **G** **D**
Ever since I put your pic - ture in a frame.

Rain Dogs

Words & Music by Tom Waits

Intro | C♯7 *ad lib. accordian cadenza*   D | G♯7 | C♯7   ‖

Verse 1

F♯m
   Inside a broken clock, splashing the wine,

         G
With all the Rain Dogs.

F♯m
   Taxi, we'd rather walk.

               G
Huddle a doorway with the Rain Dogs.

C♯7   F♯m
   For I am a Rain Dog too.

Bridge 1

C♯7   F♯m
   Oh, how we danced and we swallowed the night,

C♯7   F♯m
   For it was all ripe for dreaming.

C♯7   F♯m
   Oh, how we danced away all of the lights,

       Bm   F♯m   G♯7   C♯7
We've always been out of our minds.

Verse 2

F♯m
   The rum pours strong and thin,

             G
Beat out the dustman with the Rain Dogs.

F♯m
   Aboard a shipwreck train,

            G
Give my umbrella to the Rain Dogs.

C♯7   F♯m
   For I am a Rain Dog too.

Bridge 2

C♯7   F♯m
Oh, how we danced with the Rose of Tralee,
C♯7   F♯m
Her long hair black as a raven.
C♯7   F♯m
Oh, how we danced and you whispered to me,
  Bm F♯m G♯7 C♯7
You'll never be going back home.

Bridge 3

C♯7   F♯m
Oh, how we danced with the Rose of Tralee,
C♯7   F♯m
Her long hair black as a raven.
C♯7   F♯m
Oh, how we danced and you whispered to me,
  Bm F♯m G♯7 C♯7 F♯m
You'll never be going back home.   *To fade*

Rains On Me

Words & Music by Tom Waits & Chuck E. Weiss

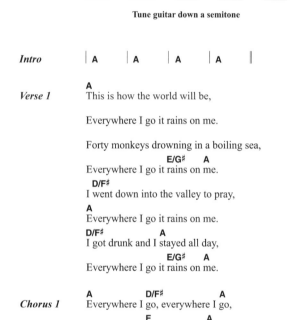

Tune guitar down a semitone

Intro | A | A | A | A   ‖

Verse 1
A
This is how the world will be,

Everywhere I go it rains on me.

Forty monkeys drowning in a boiling sea,
                          E/G♯   A
Everywhere I go it rains on me.
  D/F♯
I went down into the valley to pray,
A
Everywhere I go it rains on me.
D/F♯   A
I got drunk and I stayed all day,
                 E/G♯   A
Everywhere I go it rains on me.

Chorus 1
A   D/F♯   A
Everywhere I go, everywhere I go,
               E   A
Everywhere I go, it rains on me.

Verse 2

A
All God's children can't you see,

   E/G♯ **A**
Everywhere I go it rains on me.

Louie Lista and Marchese,

   E/G♯ **A**
Everywhere I go it rains on me.

D/F♯   **A**
Robert Sheehan and Paul Body,

   E/G♯ **A**
Everywhere I go it rains on me.

D/F♯
I went down to Argyle, I went down to Dix,

A
Everywhere I go it rains on me.

  D/F♯   **A**
To get my special powders and to get my fix,

   E/G♯ **A**
Everywhere I go it rains on me.

Chorus 2 As Chorus 1

   A   **D/F♯**   **A**
Chorus 3 And everywhere I go, everywhere I go,

     E/G♯ **A**
Everywhere I go, it rains on me.

     D/F♯   **A**
Everywhere I go, everywhere I go,

     E/G♯   **D/F♯** **A6**
Everywhere I go, it rains on me. Ooh.

On The Nickel

Words & Music by Tom Waits

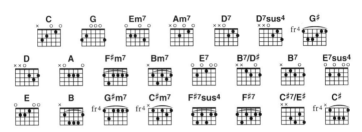

Tune guitar down a semitone

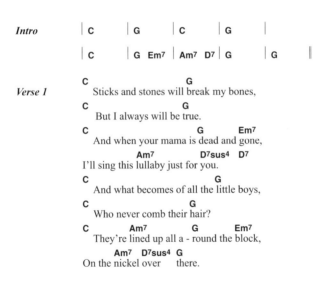

Intro

| C | G | C | G | |

| C | G Em7 | Am7 D7 | G | G | ‖

Verse 1

    C   G
Sticks and stones will break my bones,

    C   G
 But I always will be true.

    C   G   Em7
And when your mama is dead and gone,

           Am7   D7sus4 D7
I'll sing this lullaby just for you.

    C   G
And what becomes of all the little boys,

    C   G
 Who never comb their hair?

    C   Am7   G   Em7
 They're lined up all a - round the block,

           Am7   D7sus4 G
On the nickel over   there.

C   G
So you better bring a bucket,

C   G
There is a hole in the pail.

C   G   Em⁷
And if you don't get my let - ter,

            Am⁷   D⁷sus⁴ D⁷
Then you'll know that I'm in jail.

C   G
And what becomes of all the little boys,

C   G
Who never say their prayers?

C   Am⁷   G   Em⁷
They're sleeping like a ba - by,

         Am⁷ D⁷sus⁴ G
On the nickel over   there.

    | C | G♯ | D | A   ‖

D   A
And if you chew to - bacco,

D   A
And wish upon a star,

D   A   F♯m⁷
You'll find out where the scare - crows sit,

           Bm⁷   E⁷
Just like punchlines between the cars.

D   A
And I know a place where a royal flush,

D   A
Can never beat a pair.

D   B⁷/D♯   A   F♯m⁷
And even Thomas Jeffer - son,

        Bm⁷   E⁷   A
Is on the nickel over there.

D   A
So ring around the Rosie,

D   A
Sleeping in the rain.

D   A   F♯m⁷
You're always late for sup - per,

        Bm⁷   E⁷sus⁴ E⁷
Man, you let me down, let me down again.

cont.

D   A
I thought I heard a mockingbird,

D   A
Roosevelt knows where.

D   B7/D♯   A   F♯m7
You can skip the light with Grady Tuck,

        Bm7   E7   A
On the nickel over there.

Interlude | D | A♯ | E | B   ‖

Verse 5

E   B
So what becomes of all the little boys,

E   B
Who run away from home?

E   B   G♯m7
The world just keeps getting big - ger,

        C♯m7   F♯7sus4 F♯7
Once you get out on your own.

E   B
So here's to all the little boys,

E   B
The sandman takes you where,

E   B   G♯m7
You'll be sleeping with a pillow - man,

        C♯m7 F♯7 B
On the nickel over there.

Verse 6

E   B
So climb up through that button hole,

E   B
Fall right up the stairs.

E   C♯7/E♯   B   G♯m7
I'll show you where the short dogs grow,

        C♯m7 F♯7 B
On the nickel over there.

Outro | E | G♯ | C♯ | G♯   ‖

Road To Peace

Words & Music by Tom Waits & Kathleen Brennan

Intro | Am E⁷ | Am E⁷ | Am E⁷ | Am E⁷ ‖

Verse 1

Am E⁷ Am E⁷ Am E⁷   Am E⁷
Young Ab - del Mah - di Shab - neh was only eighteen years old,

  Am E⁷ Am E⁷
He was the youngest of nine children,

   Am   E⁷ Am E⁷
He never spent a night a - way from home.

    Dm
And his mother held his photograph up,

E⁷   Am
In the New York Times,

 E⁷ Am E⁷ Am E⁷
To see the killing has in - tensified,

   Am E⁷ Am E⁷ Am E⁷ Am E⁷
A - long the road to peace.

Verse 2

 E⁷ Am E⁷   Am   E⁷
He was a tall, thin boy with a wispy mou - stache,

  Am E⁷ Am E⁷
Dis - guised as an orthodox Jew.

  Am E⁷ Am   E⁷
On a crowded bus in Je - rusalem,

     Am   E⁷
Some had sur - vived World War Two.

   Dm
And the thunderous explosion,

   E⁷   Am
Blew out windows two-hundred yards a - way.

E⁷   Am E⁷ Am E⁷
 With more retri - bution and seventeen dead,

  Am E⁷ Am E⁷ Am E⁷
A - long the road to peace.

Verse 3

E⁷   Am   E⁷ Am   E⁷
Now at King George Ave.   and Jaffa Road,

        Am   E⁷   Am E⁷
Passeng - ers boarded bus Fourteen A.

Am E⁷   Am   E⁷   Am   E⁷   E⁷
In the aisle next to the driver   Ab - del Mahdi Shab - neh.

    Dm
And the last thing that he said on earth is:

    E⁷   Am
"God is great and God is good."

E⁷   Am   Am   E⁷
And he blew them all to kingdom come,

   Am   E⁷   Am   E⁷ Am E⁷ Am E⁷ Am E⁷
U - pon the road to peace.

Verse 4

E⁷   Am   E⁷   Am
Now in re - sponse to this an - other,

E⁷   Am   E⁷   Am   E⁷
Kiss of death was visited up - on,

     Am   E⁷ Am E⁷   Am E⁷   Am   E⁷
Yas - ser Ta - ha, Israel says is an Ha - mas senior militant.

    Dm
And Israel sent four choppers in,

      E⁷   Am
Flames en - gulfed his white O - pal.

E⁷   Am   E⁷   Am   E⁷
And it killed his wife and his three year old child,

      Am E⁷   Am   E⁷ Am E⁷ Am E⁷ Am
Leaving only blackened skeletons.

Verse 5

E⁷   Am   E⁷   Am   E⁷
They found his toddler's bottle and a pair of small shoes,

    Am   E⁷   Am   E⁷
And they waved them in front of the cameras.

  Am   E⁷   Am   E⁷
But Israel says they did not know,

    Am   E⁷   Am   E⁷
That his wife and child were in the car.

    Dm
There are roadblocks everywhere,

    E⁷   Am
And only suffering on T. - V.

E⁷   Am   E⁷   Am   E⁷
Neither side will ever give up their smallest right,

  Am   E⁷   Am   E⁷ Am E⁷
A - long the road to peace.

Am E7   Am   E7
Israel launched it's latest cam - paign,

     Am   E7   Am   E7
A - gainst Ha - mas on Tuesday.

Am   E7   Am   E7
Two days later Ha - mas shot back,

     Am   E7   Am   E7
And killed five Israeli soldiers.

     Dm
So thousands dead and wounded on both sides,

     E7   Am
Most of them Middle Eastern ci - vilians.

         Am   E7   Am   E7
They fill the children full of hate to fight an old man's war,

     Am   E7   Am   E7 Am E7
And die upon the road to peace.

E7   Am   E7   Am   E7   Am
"Now this is our land we will fight with all our force,"

E7   Am E7   Am E7
Say the Pal - estinians and the Jews.

         Am   E7   Am   E7
Each side will cut off the hand of anyone,

     Am   E7
Who tries to stop the re - sistance.

     Dm
If the right eye offends thee,

    E7   Am E7
Then you must pluck it out.

    Am   E7   Am   E7
Then Mahmoud Ab - bas said Sha - ron had been lost,

Am   E7   Am   E7 Am E7
Out along the road to peace.

E7   Am   E7   Am   E7
Once Kissinger said, "We have no friends,

    Am   E7   Am   E7
A - merica only has interests."

        Am   E7   Am   E7
Now our President wants to be seen as a hero,

       Am   E7   Am   E7
And he's hungry for re - e - lection.

     Dm
But Bush is reluctant to risk his future,

    E7   Am
In the fear of his political failures.

cont.

              E7   **Am**   **E7**
So he plays chess at his desk and poses for the press,

       Am
Ten thousand miles,

          E7   **Am**   **E7** **Am** **E7** **Am** **E7** **Am** **E7**
From the road to peace.

Verse 9

E7   **Am** **E7**   **Am**   **E7**
In the video   that they found at the home,

      Am   **E7**   **Am** **E7**
Of Ab - del Mah - di Shab - neh,

      Am   **E7**   **Am** **E7**
He held a Ka - lashnikov rifle,

         Am   **E7**   **Am** **E7**
And he spoke with a voice like a boy.

          Dm
He was an excellent student, he studied so hard,

      E7   **Am**   **E7**
It was as if he had a future.

         Am   **E7**   **Am**   **E7**
He told his mother that he had a test that day,

Am   **E7**   **Am**   **E7** **Am** **E7** **Am** **E7**
Out along the road to peace.

Verse 10

E7   **Am**   **E7**   **Am**   **E7**
The funda - mentalist killing on both sides,

     Am   **E7**   **Am** **E7**
Is standing in the path of peace.

        Am   **E7**   **Am**   **E7**
But tell me why are we arming the Israeli army,

      Am   **E7**   **Am**   **E7**
With guns and tanks and bullets?

      Dm
And if God is great and God is good,

        E7   **Am**
Why can't he change the hearts of men?

      E7   **Am**   **E7**   **Am**   **E7**
Well maybe God him - self is lost and needs help,

        Am   **E7**   **Am**   **E7**
Maybe God him - self he needs all of our help,

        Am   **E7**   **Am**   **E7**
Maybe God him - self is lost and needs help,

      Am   **E7**   **Am** **E7**
He's out upon the road to peace.

cont.

        E⁷   Am   E⁷   Am   E⁷
Well maybe God him - self is lost and needs help,

          Am   E⁷   Am   E⁷
Maybe God him - self he needs all of our help,

         Am   E⁷   Am
And he's lost upon the road to peace.

                 E⁷   Am   E⁷
And he's lost upon the road to peace.

Am   E⁷   Am   E⁷
Out upon the road to peace.

Outro | Am E⁷ | Am E⁷ | Am E⁷ | Am E⁷ | Am⁷ ||

Ruby's Arms

Words & Music by Tom Waits

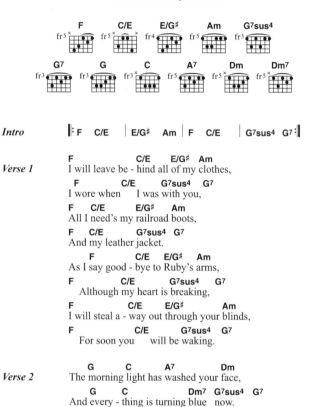

Intro　　　‖: F　C/E　|　E/G♯　Am |　F　C/E　|　G⁷sus⁴　G⁷ :‖

Verse 1
> 　　　　　F　　　　　C/E　E/G♯　Am
> I will leave be - hind all of my clothes,
>
> 　　　F　　　　C/E　　G⁷sus⁴　G⁷
> I wore when　　I was with you,
>
> 　F　C/E　　　　E/G♯　Am
> All I need's my railroad boots,
>
> F　C/E　　　　G⁷sus⁴　G⁷
> And my leather jacket.
>
> 　　　　F　　　　C/E　E/G♯　Am
> As I say good - bye to Ruby's arms,
>
> 　F　　　　C/E　　　　G⁷sus⁴　G⁷
> 　Although my heart is breaking,
>
> F　　　　C/E　　　E/G♯　　　　Am
> I will steal a - way out through your blinds,
>
> F　　　　C/E　　　　G⁷sus⁴　G⁷
> 　For soon you　　will be waking.

Verse 2
> 　　　G　　　C　　　A⁷　　　　Dm
> The morning light has washed your face,
>
> 　　　G　　　C　　　Dm⁷　G⁷sus⁴　G⁷
> And every - thing is turning blue　now.
>
> G　　C　　　A⁷　　Dm
> Hold on to your pillow case,
>
> 　　　　G　　　C　　Dm⁷　G⁷sus⁴　G⁷
> There's nothing I can do　　now.

cont.

     F   **C/E**   **E/G♯**   **Am**
As I say good - bye to Ruby's arms,

     F   **C/E** **G7sus4** **G7**
You'll find an - other soldier.

        F   **C/E**   **E/G♯**   **Am**
And I swear to God by Christmas time,

          F   **C/E** **G7sus4** **G7**
There'll be someone else to hold you.

Verse 3

     G   **C**   **A7**   **Dm**
The only thing I'm taking is,

     G   **C**   **Dm7** **G7sus4** **G7**
The scarf off of your clothes line.

     G   **C**   **A7**   **Dm**
I'll hurry past your chest of drawers,

G   **C**   **Dm7** **G7sus4** **G7**
And your broken wind chimes.

     F   **C/E**   **E/G♯**   **Am**
As I say good - bye, I'll say good - bye,

          Dm7 **G7sus4** **G7** **(F)**
Say good - bye to Ru   -   by's arms.

Instrumental | **F** **C/E** | **E/G♯** **Am** | **F** **C/E** | **G7sus4** **G7** | **C** ‖

Verse 4

     F   **C/E**   **E/G♯**   **Am**
I will feel my way down the darkened hall,

     F   **C/E** **G7sus4** **G7**
And out in - to the morning.

     F   **C/E** **E/G♯**   **Am**
The hobos at the freight - yards,

       F   **C/E** **G7sus4**   **G7**
Have kept their fires burning.

     F   **C/E**   **E/G♯**   **Am**
So Jesus Christ this goddam rain,

     F   **C/E**   **E/G♯** **Am**
Will someone put me on a train.

        F **C/E**   **E/G♯**   **Am**
I'll nev - er kiss your lips a - gain,

    Dm7 **G7sus4**   **G7**
Or break your heart.

     F   **C/E**   **E/G♯**   **Am**
As I say good - bye, I'll say good - bye,

          Dm7 **G7sus4** **G7** **(F)**
Say good - bye to Ru   -   by's arms.

San Diego Serenade

Words & Music by Tom Waits

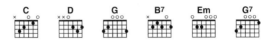

C   D   G   B7   Em   G7

Tune guitar down a semitone

Intro

| C D | G | C D | G ||

Verse 1

G   B7   Em   G7
I never saw the morning till I stayed up all night,
C   D   G   B7 Em G7 C
   I never saw the sunshine till you turned out the light.
                      D   G   B7 Em G7 C
I never saw my hometown until I stayed away   too long,
                      D   C   D G
I never heard the melody until I needed the song.

Link 1

| C D | G | C D | G ||

Verse 2

G   B7   Em   G7
I never saw the white line, till I was leaving you behind,
C   D   G   B7 Em G7
   I never knew I needed you until I was caught up in a bind.
          D   G   B7 Em G7 C
I never spoke I love you till I cursed you in   vain,
                    D   C   D G
I never felt my heartstrings until I nearly went in - sane.

Link 2

| C D | G | C D | G ||

Verse 2

```
         G        B7                      Em                      G7
         I never saw the east coast until I    moved to the west,
         C              D                    G            B7    Em G7 C
           I never saw the moonlight until it shone off of your breast.
                        D              G
         I never saw your heart until someone   tried to steal,
         B7              Em    G7  C
           Tried to steal it a - way,
                          D            C          D   G
         I never saw your tears until they rolled down your face.
```

Link 3 | C D | G | C D | G   ‖

Verse 3

```
         G        B7               Em                  G7
         I never saw the morning till   I stayed up all night,
         C              D                    G            B7    Em G7 C
           I never saw the sunshine till you turned out your lovelight baby.
                      D           G          B7   Em   G7 C
         I never saw my hometown until   I stayed away   too long,
                      D          C       D  G
         I never heard the melody until I needed the song.
```

Outro | C D | G | C D | G | C D | G   ‖

Romeo Is Bleeding

Words & Music by Tom Waits

Bm7 fr7

F#9 fr8

Intro ‖: Bm7 | F#9 | Bm7 | F#9 :‖

Verse 1

Bm7   F#9
Romeo is bleeding but not so as you'd notice,
     Bm7   F#9
He's over on 18th Street as usu - al.
Bm7   F#9
Looking so hard against the hood of his car,
     Bm7   F#9
And putting out a cigarette in his hand.
                    Bm7
And for all the pa - chucos at the pumps,

        F#9
At Ro - meros Paint and Body,

                    Bm7
They all seeing how far they can spit,

           F#9
Well it was just another night.

                 Bm7   F#9
And now they're huddled in the brake lights of a '58 Belair,
     Bm7   F#9
And listening to how Romeo killed a sheriff with his knife.
                 Bm7
And they all jump when they hear the sirens,
     F#9
But Romeo just laughs and says,

            Bm7
"All the racket in the world ain't never gonna
F#9
Save that copper's ass.

          Bm7
He ain't never gonna see another summertime
   F#9
For gunnin' down my brother."

cont.

Bm⁷
And leaving him like a dog,

F♯9
Beneath a car without his knife.

Bm⁷
Romeo says, "Hey man, gimme a cigarette."

F♯9
And they hurry for their pack.

Bm⁷   **F♯9**
And Frankie lights it for him and pats him on the back,

Bm⁷
And throws a bottle at a milk truck,

F♯9
And as it breaks he grabs his nuts.

Bm⁷
And they all know they'd get bitches like Romeo,

F♯9
If they only had the guts.

Bm⁷   **F♯9**
Verse 2 But Romeo is bleeding but nobody can tell,

Bm⁷
He sings along with the radio,

F♯9
With a bullet in his chest.

Bm⁷
And he combs back his fenders,

F♯9
And they all agree it's clear,

Bm⁷   **F♯9**
That everything is cool now that Romeo is here.

Bm⁷
But Romeo is bleeding,

F♯9
And he winces now and then,

Bm⁷
And he leans against the car door,

F♯9
And feels the blood in his shoes.

Bm⁷
And someone's crying at the fire point,

F♯9
In the phone booth by the store.

Bm⁷
Romeo starts his engines,

F♯9   **Bm⁷ F♯9**
And wipes the blood off the door.

163

cont.

Bm⁷
And he brodys through the signal,

F♯9
With the radio full blast,

Bm⁷   F♯9
Leaving the boys there hiking up their chinos.

Bm⁷
And then they all try to stand like Romeo,

F♯9
Beneath the moon cut like a sickle,

Bm⁷   F♯9
And they're talking now in Spanish all a - bout their hero.

Sax. solo   ‖: Bm⁷ | F♯9 | Bm⁷ | F♯9 :‖ *Play 7 times*

              | Bm⁷ | F♯9 ‖

Verse 3

Bm⁷   F♯9
Romeo is bleeding as he gives the man his ticket,

Bm⁷   F♯9
And he climbs to the balcony at the movies.

Bm⁷
And he'll die without a whimper,

F♯9
Like every hero's dream.

Bm⁷
Like an angel with a bullet,

F♯9
And Cagney on the screen.

Bm⁷   F♯9
Romeo is bleeding.

Bm⁷   F♯9
Romeo is bleeding.

Bm⁷   F♯9
Romeo is bleeding,   hey man.

Outro   ‖: Bm⁷ | F♯9 | Bm⁷ | F♯9 :‖ *Ad lib. vocals to fade*

Shiver Me Timbers

Words & Music by Tom Waits

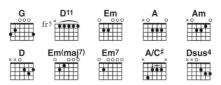

Tune guitar down a semitone

Intro | G D11 | G Em | G A | Am D | G ‖

Verse 1

G   D11
I'm leaving my family,

G   Em
I'm leaving all my friends.

G   A
  My body's at home,

       Am   D
But my heart's in the wind,

            G   D11
Where the clouds are like headlines,

          G   Em
On a new front-page sky.

G   A
  My tears are salt water,

       Am   D   G
And the moon's full and high.

Verse 2

G   D11
And I know Martin Eden's,

         G   Em
Gonna be proud of me   now,

G   A
   And many be - fore me,

              Am   D
Who've been called by the sea.

              G   D11
To be up in the crow's nest,

G   Em
Singing my say,

G   A
Shiver me timbers,

                Am   D G
'Cause I'm a - sailing a - way.

Bridge 1

G   Em
And the fog's lifting,

        Em(maj7)
And the sand's shifting,

Em7   A/C♯
I'm drifting on out.

A
Old Captain Ahab,

          Dsus4   D
He ain't got nothing on me, now.

Em   Em(maj7)
  So swallow me, don't follow me,

Em7   A/C♯
  I'm travelling alone.

     A
Blue water's my daughter,

           Dsus4   D   (G)
And I'm gonna skip like a stone._____

Solo | G D11 | G Em | G A | Am D | G   ‖

Verse 3

```
G                    D11
So please call my missus,
G                         Em
   Got to tell her not to cry.
G                        A
   'Cause my goodbye is written,
      Am          D
By the moon in the sky.
              G              D11
Hey and nobody knows me,
       G              Em
I can't fathom my stay - ing,
G          A
   Shiver me timbers,
                Am    D  G
'Cause I'm a - sailing a - way.
```

Bridge 2   As Bridge 1

Verse 4
```
            G                 D11
And I'm leaving my family,
G                  Em
   I'm leaving all my friends.
G                A
   My body's at home,
      Am          D
But my heart's in the wind,
             G              D11
Where the clouds are like headlines,
         G               A
Upon a new front-page sky.
G                A
   And shiver me timbers,
             Am    D (G)
'Cause I'm a - sailing a - way.
```

Outro   ‖ G D11 │ G Em │ G A │ Am D │ G   ‖

A Sight For Sore Eyes

Words & Music by Tom Waits

C   G   F   Am   Dm

Intro	C	G	C	F	
	C	G	Am F G C		

Verse 1

C   F   C
A sight for sore eyes, it's a long-time no-see,

                Am   Dm   G
Working hard, hardly working, hey man, you know me.

          C   F   C
Water under the bridge, did you see my new car?

               Am   Dm   G
Well it's bought and it's payed for, parked out - side of the bar.

Chorus 1

(G)   C   F   C
And hey bar-keeper, what's keeping you? Keep pouring drinks,

                Am   Dm   G
For all these pa - lookas, hey you know what I thinks.

             C   F   C
That we toast to the old days and Di - maggio too,

                Am   Dm   G (C)
And old Drysdale and Mantle, Whitey Ford and to you.

Link 1	C	C	F	C	
	C	Am	Dm G	C	G

Verse 2

```
      (G)    C                          F            C
No the old gang ain't around, every - one has left town,
                          Am           Dm            G
'Cept for Thumm and Giar - dina said they just might be down.
             C                    F            C
Oh, half-drunk all the time and I'm all-drunk the rest,
                          Am           Dm    G
Yeah, Monk's still the champion, oh, but I am the best.
```

Chorus 2   As Chorus 1

Link 2   As Link 1

Verse 3

```
      (G)    C                          F            C
Guess you heard about Nash, he was killed in a crash,
                          Am           Dm    G
Oh, that must of been two or three years ago now.
             C                    F            C
Heard he spun out and he rolled, hit a telephone pole,
                          Am  Dm  G
And he died with the radio on.
             C                    F            C
No, she's married with a kid, finally split up with Sid,
                          Am           Dm            G
He's up north for a nickel's worth for armed robbe - ry.
             C                    F            C
And I'll play you some pinball, no you ain't got a chance,
                          Am    Dm    G
Then go on over and ask her to dance.
```

Chorus 3

```
      (G)    C                          F            C
And hey bar-keep, what's keeping you? Keep pouring drinks,
                          Am           Dm            G
For all these pa - lookas, hey you know what I thinks.
             C                    F            C
That we toast to the old days and Di - maggio too,
                          Am           Dm       G (C)
And Drysdale and Mantle, Whitey Ford and to  you.
```

Outro

```
| C         | C         | F         | C         |

| C         | Am        | Dm   G    | C         ‖
```

Sins Of The Father

Words & Music by Tom Waits & Kathleen Brennan

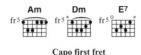

Capo first fret

Intro | Am | Am | Am | Am |

Verse 1
Am
God said don't give me your tin-horn prayers,

And don't buy roses off the street down there.
Dm
  Took it all and took the dirt road home,

Am
Dreaming of Jenny with the light brown hair.
E7   **Am**
  Night is falling like a bloody axe,
E7   **Am**
  Lies and rumours and the wind at my back.
E7   **Am**
  Hand on the wheel gravel on the road,
         E7
Will the pawn shop sell me back what I sold?

Chorus 1
            Am
I'm gonna take the sins of my father,
            Am   **E7**
I'm gonna take the sins of my mother,
            Am
I'm gonna take the sins of my brother,
    E7   **Am**
Down to the pond.

Verse 2

Am
Birds cry warning from a hidden branch,

Carving out a future with a gun and an axe.

Dm
I'm way beyond the gavel and the laws of man,

Am
Still living in the palm of the grace of your hand.

E7   **Am**
  The world's not easy, the blind man said,

E7   **Am**
  Turns on nothing but money and dread.

E7   **Am**
  Dogs been scratching at the door all night,

E7
Long neck birds flying out of the moonlight.

Chorus 2

          Am
I'm gonna take the sins of my father,

                      E7
I'm gonna take the sins of my mother,

          Am
I'm gonna take the sins of my brother,

    E7   **Am**
Down to the pond.

    E7   **Am**
Down to the pond.

Verse 3

Am
Smack dab in the middle of a dirty lie,

The star spangled glitter of his one good eye.

Dm
Everybody knows that the game was rigged,

Am
Justice wears suspenders and a powdered wig.

E7   **Am**
  Dark town alleys been hiding you,

E7   **Am**
  Long bell tolling is your Waterloo.

E7   **Am**
  Oh baby what can you do,

       E7
Does the light of God blind you,

Or lead the way home for you?

Chorus 3

          Am
I'm gonna take the sins of my father,

              E7
Take the sins of my mother,

          Am
I'm gonna take the sins of my brother,

   E7   **Am**
Down to the pond.

   E7   **Am**
Down to the pond.

Guitar solo

‖: **Am** | **Am** | **Am** | **Am** :‖

| **Dm** | **Dm** | **Dm** | **Dm** |

| **Am** | **Am** | **Am** | **Am** |

| **E7 Am** | **E7 Am** | **E7 Am** | **E7** | **E7** ‖

Chorus 4

          Am
I'm gonna take the sins of my father,

              E7
Take the sins of my mother,

   Am
And take the sins of my brother,

   E7   **Am**
Down to the pond.

   E7   **Am**
Down to the pond.

Verse 4

Am
God almighty for righteousness sake,

Humiliation of our fallen state.

Dm
Written in the book of Tubal Cain,

   Am
A long black overcoat will show no stain.

E7   **Am**
  Feel the heat and the burn on your back,

E7   **Am**
  The rip and the moan and the stretch of the rack.

E7   **Am**
  All my belongings in a flour sack,

     E7
Will the place I come from take me back?

Chorus 5

        Am
I'm gonna take the sins of my father,
              E7
Take the sins of my mother,
        Am
And take the sins of my brother,
       E7   **Am**
Down to the pond.
       E7   **Am**
Down to the pond.

Verse 5

Am
They'll hang me in the morning on a scaffold yea big,

To dance upon nothing to the Tyburn jig.
Dm
Treats you like a puppet when you're under its spell,
      Am
Oh the heart is heaven but the mind is hell.
E7   **Am**
   Jesus of Nazareth told Mike of the weeds,
E7   **Am**
   I's born at this time for a reason you see,
E7   **Am**
   When I'm dead I'll be dead a long time,
       E7
But the wine's so pleasing and so sublime.

Chorus 6

        Am
I'm gonna take the sins of my father,
             E7
And take the sins of my mother,
        Am
I'm gonna take the sins of my brother,
      E7   **Am**
Down to the pond.
      E7   **Am**
Down to the pond.

Verse 6

Am
Kissed my sweetheart by the chinaball tree,

Everything I done is between God and me.

Dm
  Only he will judge how my time was spent,

Am
Twenty-nine days of sinning and forty to repent.

E7   **Am**
  The horse is steady but the horse is blind,

E7   **Am**
  Wicked are the branches on the tree of mankind.

E7   **Am**
  The roots grow upward and the branches grow down,

E7
  It's much too late to throw the dice again I've found.

Chorus 7

                  Am
I'm gonna take the sins of my father,

                      E7
Take the sins of my mother,

                  Am
I'm gonna take the sins of my brother,

        E7   **Am**
Down to the pond.

Outro

Am
I'm gonna wash them.

I'm gonna wash them.

I'm gonna wash the sins of my father,

                          E7
I'm gonna wash the sins of my mother,

Am
Wash the sins of my brother,

Till the water runs clear,

Till the water runs clear,

Till the water runs clear.

16 Shells From A Thirty-Ought Six

Words & Music by Tom Waits

Intro

‖: C♯m | C♯m | C♯m | C♯m :‖

Verse 1

C♯m
    I plugged sixteen shells from a thirty-ought-six,

And a Black Crow snuck through a hole in the sky.
    F♯5
So I spent all my buttons on an old pack mule,
    C♯m
And I made me a ladder from a pawnshop marimba,
    G♯m7
And I leaned it up against a dandelion tree.
F♯5
Leaned it up against a dandelion tree.

C♯m
Leaned it up against a dandelion tree.

Verse 2

(C♯m)
Gonna cook them feathers on a tire iron spit.

And I filled me a satchel full of old pig corn.
    F♯5
And I beat me a billy from an old French horn,
    C♯m
And I kicked that mule to the top of the tree,

Kicked that mule to the top of the tree.
    G♯m7   **F♯5**
And I blew me a hole 'bout the size of a kick - drum,
    C♯m
And I cut me a switch from a long branch elbow.

Chorus 1

(C♯m)
I'm gonna whittle you into kindling,

Black Crow, sixteen shells from a thirty-ought-six.

Whittle you into kindling,

Black Crow, sixteen shells from a thirty-ought-six.

Verse 3

(C♯m)
Well I slept in the holler of a dry creek bed,

And I tore out the buckets from a red Corvette,

Tore out the buckets from a red Corvette.
F♯5
Lionel and Dave and the Butcher made three,
          C♯m
Ah, you got to meet me by the knuckles of the skinnybone tree.
          G♯m7   F♯5
With the strings of a Washburn stretched like a clothes line,
          C♯m
You know me and that mule scrambled right through the hole.

Me and that mule scrambled right through the hole.

Chorus 2   As Chorus 1

Verse 4

(C♯m)
Now I hold him prisoner in a Washburn jail,

That I strapped on the back of my old kick mule,

Strapped it on the back of my old kick mule.
   F♯5
I bang on the strings just to drive him crazy,
          C♯m
Oh, I strum it a-loud to rattle his cage.

Strum it a-loud just to rattle his cage.
G♯m7
Strum it a-loud just to rattle his cage,
F♯5   C♯m
Strum it a-loud just to rattle his cage.

Chorus 3	**(C♯m)** Oh, I'm gonna whittle you into kindling,
	Black Crow, sixteen shells from a thirty-ought-six.
	Whittle you into kindling,
	Black Crow, sixteen shells from a thirty-ought-six.

Outro   ‖: **C♯m** │ **C♯m** │ **C♯m** │ **C♯m** :‖ *Repeat to fade*

Soldier's Things

Words & Music by Tom Waits

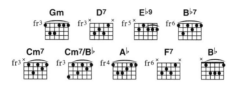

Intro
‖: Gm | D7 | Gm | D7 :‖

Verse 1

Gm   D7
Davenports and kettle drums,

Gm   D7
And swallow tail coats,

Gm   D7   E♭9   D7
Table cloths and patent leather shoes.

Gm   D7
Bathing suits and bowling balls,

Gm   D7
And clarinets and rings,

B♭7   Cm7   Cm7/B♭ A♭   D7
All this radio really needs   is a fuse.

Chorus 1

Cm7   F7
A tink - er, a tailor,

B♭7   Gm
A sold - ier's things,

Cm7   F7   B♭7 D7
His rifle, his boots full of rocks.

   Gm   D7
Oh, and this one is for bravery,

Gm   E♭9
And this one is for me,

D7   Gm D7   Gm D7
And everything's a dollar in   this box.

Verse 2

Gm   **D7**
Cuff links and hub caps,

Gm   **D7**
Trophies and paperbacks.

Gm   **B♭**
It's good transport - ation,

E♭9   **D7**
But the brakes aren't so hot.

Gm   **D7**
Neck ties and boxing gloves,

Gm   **D7**
This jackknife is rusted,

B♭7   **Cm7** **Cm7/B♭** **A♭**   **D7**
You can pound that dent out   on the hood.

Chorus 2   As Chorus 1

Outro | **Gm** | **D7** | **Gm** ‖

Step Right Up

Words & Music by Tom Waits

No chords in this song

Bass arr. for guitar

riff 1

Intro

Bb	Bb	C	Db	D	F	Ab	A	Bb	Bb	C	Db	D	Db	C	B
3fr	1fr	3fr	4fr	5fr	3fr	1fr	2fr	3fr	1fr	3fr	4fr	5fr	6fr	5fr	4fr
③	⑤	⑤	⑤	⑤	④	③	③	③	⑤	⑤	⑤	⑤	③	③	③

Verse

riff 1 *throughout*
Step right up, step right up, step right up,

Everyone's a winner, bargains galore.

That's right, you too can be the proud owner,

Of the quality goes in before the name goes on.

One-tenth of a dollar, one-tenth of a dollar,

We got service after sales.

How 'bout perfume? We got perfume,

How 'bout an engagement ring?

Something for the little lady, something for the little lady,

Something for the little lady, hmm.

Three for a dollar.

We got a year-end clearance, we got a white sale,

And a smoke-damaged furniture, you can drive it away today.

Act now, act now, and receive as our gift, our gift to you,

They come in all colors, one size fits all.

No muss, no fuss, no spills, you're tired of kitchen drudgery,

Everything must go, going out of business, going out of business,

Going out of business sale.

Fifty percent off original retail price, skip the middleman,

Don't settle for less.

How do we do it? How do we do it?

Volume, volume, turn up the volume.

Now you've heard it advertised, don't hesitate,

Don't be caught with your drawers down,

Don't be caught with your drawers down.

You can step right up, step right up.

That's right, it fillets, it chops, it dices, slices,

Never stops, lasts a lifetime, mows your lawn,

And it mows your lawn and it picks up the kids from school,

It gets rid of unwanted facial hair, it gets rid of embarrassing age spots,

It delivers a pizza, and it lengthens, and it strengthens,

And it finds that slipper that's been at large,

Under the chaise lounge for several weeks.

And it plays a mean Rhythm Master,

It makes excuses for unwanted lipstick on your collar,

And it's only a dollar, step right up, it's only a dollar, step right up.

cont.   'Cause it forges your signature,

If not completely satisfied, mail back unused portion of product,

For complete refund of price of purchase.

Step right up.

Please allow thirty days for delivery,

Don't be fooled by cheap imitations,

You can live in it, live in it, laugh in it, love in it,

Swim in it, sleep in it,

Live in it, swim in it, laugh in it, love in it.

Removes embarrassing stains from contour sheets, that's right.

And it entertains visiting relatives, it turns a sandwich into a banquet,

Tired of being the life of the party?

Change your shorts, change your life, change your life,

Change into a nine-year-old Hindu boy, get rid of your wife,

And it walks your dog, and it doubles on sax,

Doubles on sax, you can jump back Jack, see you later alligator,

See you later alligator and it steals your car.

It gets rid of your gambling debts, it quits smoking,

It's a friend, it's a companion,

It's the only product you will ever need.

Follow these easy assembly instructions, it never needs ironing.

Well, it takes weights off hips, bust, thighs, chin, midriff,

Gives you dandruff, and it finds you a job, it is a job.

And it strips the phone company free take ten for five exchange,

And it gives you denture breath.

And you know it's a friend, and it's a companion,

And it gets rid of your traveller's checks.

It's new, it's improved, it's old-fashioned,

Well it takes care of business, never needs winding,

Never needs winding, never needs winding.

Gets rid of blackheads, the heartbreak of psoriasis,

Christ, you don't know the meaning of heartbreak, buddy,

C'mon, c'mon, c'mon, c'mon.

'Cause it's effective, it's defective, it creates household odours,

It disinfects, it sanitizes for your protection,

It gives you an erection, it wins the election.

Why put up with painful corns any longer?

It's a redeemable coupon, no obligation,

No salesman will visit your home.

We got a jackpot, jackpot, jackpot, prizes, prizes, prizes,

All work guaranteed.

How do we do it, how do we do it, how do we do it, how do we do it?

We need your business, we're going out of business,

We'll give you the business.

Get on the business end of our going-out-of-business sale.

Receive our free brochure, free brochure.

cont.   Read the easy-to-follow assembly instructions, batteries not included.

Send before midnight tomorrow, terms available,

Step right up, step right up, step right up.

You got it buddy: the large print giveth,

And the small print taketh away.

Step right up, you can step right up, you can step right up,

C'mon step right up.

(Get away from me kid, you're bothering me...)

Step right up, step right up, step right up.

C'mon, c'mon, c'mon, c'mon, c'mon,

Step right up, you can step right up, c'mon and step right up,

C'mon and step right up.

riff 1 *(x2) to finish*

A Sweet Little Bullet
From A Pretty Blue Gun

Words & Music by Tom Waits

Am   F#m7♭5   E   F#m   Gm   G#m   Am7

Intro | Am7 | Am7 | Am7 | Am7 |

Verse 1

Am
Well it's raining, it's pouring,

And you didn't bring a sweater,
              F#m7♭5   E   F#m Gm G#m
Nebraska will never let you come back home.
        Am
And on Hollywood and Vine,

By the Thrifty Mart sign,
                    F#m7♭5   E   F#m Gm G#m
Any night I'll be willing to bet,
          Am
There's a young girl,

With sweet little dreams and pretty blue wishes,
              F#m7♭5 E   Am
Standing there   just getting all wet.

Verse 2

Am7
Now there's a place off the drag,

Called the Gilbert Hotel,
                    F#m7♭5   E   F#m Gm G#m
And there's a couple letters burned out in the sign.
          Am7
And it's better than a bus stop,

And they do good business every time it rains.

For little girls with nothing in their jeans,
F#m7♭5   E   Am7
But pretty blue wishes and sweet little dreams.

Verse 3

Am7
And it's raining, it's pouring.

The old man is snoring,

Now I lay me down to sleep.

I hear the sirens in the street,

All my dreams are made of chrome,

F#m7♭5   E   F#m Gm
I have no way to get back home.

G#m Am7
I'd   rather die before I wake,

            F#m7♭5
Like Marilyn Monroe.

            Am7
And you can throw my dreams out in the street,

            F#m7♭5 E   Am7
And let the rain   make them grow.

Sax. solo

Am7	Am7	Am7	Am7
Am7	F#m7♭5	E F#m	Gm G#m
Am7	Am7	Am7	F#m7♭5
Am7	F#m7♭5 E	Am7	Am7 ‖

Verse 4

Am7
Now the night clerk, he got a club foot,

He's heard every hard luck story,

            F#m7♭5   E   F#m Gm G#m
At least a hundred times or more.

            Am7
He says check out time is 10 a.m.,

And that's just what he means.

Go on up the stairs,

            F#m7♭5
With your sweet little wishes,

            E   Am7
And your pretty blue dreams.

Verse 5

Am7
And it's raining, it's pouring,
         F♯m7♭5
Hollywood's just fine.
Am7
Swindle a little girl out of her dreams,
      F♯m7♭5   E   F♯m Gm G♯m
Another letter in the sign.
     Am7
Now never trust a scarecrow,

Wearing shades after dark,
            F♯m7♭5
Be careful of that old bow tie he wears.
     Am7
It takes a sweet little bullet,

From a pretty blue gun,
        F♯m7♭5   E   Am7
To put those scarlet ribbons in your hair.

Guitar solo ‖: Am7 | Am7 | Am7 | Am7 :‖

Verse 6

Am7
No, that ain't no cherry bomb,
        F♯m7♭5
Fourth of July's all done.
       Am7
It's just some fool playing that second line,
    F♯m7♭5   E   Am7
From the barrel of a pretty blue gun.

No, that ain't no cherry bomb,
         F♯m7♭5
Fourth of July's all done.
   Am7
Just some fool playing that second line,
    F♯m7♭5   E   Am7
From the barrel of a pretty blue gun.

Outro ‖: Am7 | Am7 | Am7 | F♯m7♭5 |

      | Am7 | Am7 | F♯m7♭5 E | Am7 :‖ *Repeat to fade*

Strange Weather

Words & Music by Tom Waits & Kathleen Brennan

Am13 E9 Dm7 G Bm7♭5

E7 Cmaj7 Am7 A7 B7

Intro | Am13 | E9 | Am13 | E9 |

| Am13 E9 | Am13 E9 | Am13 E9 | Am13 E9 | Am13 E9 | Am13 E9 ‖

Verse 1

(E9)　　Am13　　E9　　Am13
Will you take me a - cross the Channel,

E9　　Dm7　　G　　Bm7♭5
London Bridge is falling down.

E7　　Am13　E9　　Am13
Strange a woman tries to save,

　　　　Dm7　　G　　Bm7♭5　E7
More than a man who tries to drown.

　　　　Dm7　　G　Cmaj7　Am7
And it's the rain that they pre - dicted,

　　Bm7♭5　E7　Am7
It's the forecast every time.

　　A7　　Dm7　　　　Cmaj7
The rose has died because you picked it,

　　Am7　B7　　　　E9
And I be - lieve that brandy's mine.

Chorus 1

(E9)　　A　　G
And all over the world,

F　　　E9　　　A　　G
Strangers talk only about the weather.

　　F　　　　B7
All over the world it's the same,

E7　　(Am13)
It's the same, it's the same.

Link 1 | Am13 | E9 | Am13 | E9 ‖

Verse 2

(E9)   **Am**¹³   **E9**   **Am**⁷
And the world is getting flatter,

E9   **Dm**⁷ **G**   **Bm**⁷♭⁵
And the sky is falling all around.

E⁷   **Am**⁷   **E9**   **Am**¹³
  Oh, and nothing is the matter,

    Dm⁷ **G**   **Bm**⁷♭⁵ **E**⁷
For I never cry in town.

     Dm⁷   **G** **Cmaj**⁷
And a love like ours, my dear,

Am⁷ **Bm**⁷♭⁵   **E**⁷   **Am**⁷
Is best measured when its down.

A⁷   **Dm**⁷   **Cmaj**⁷
And I never buy um - brellas,

Am⁷   **B**⁷   **E9**
  'Cause there's always one a - round.

Chorus 2

(E9)   **A**   **G**
And all over the world

F   **E9**   **A**   **G**
Strangers talk only about the weather.

  F   **B**⁷
All over the world it's the same,

E⁷   (**Am**¹³)
It's the same.

Link 2

| **Am**¹³ | **E9** | **Am**¹³ | **E9**   ‖

Bridge

(E9)   **Dm**⁷   **Cmaj**⁷
And you know that it's be - ginning,

Am⁷   **Bm**⁷♭⁵   **E**⁷   **Am**⁷
  And you know that it's the end.

     Dm⁷   **Cmaj**⁷
Once a - gain we are strangers,

Am⁷ **B**⁷   **E9**
  As the fog goes rolling in.

Chorus 3

(E9)   **A**   **G**
And all over the world,

F   **E9**   **A**   **G**
Strangers talk only about the weather.

  F   **B**⁷
All over the world it's the same,

E⁷ **Am**¹³   **E9** **Am**¹³
It's the same,

E9   **Am**¹³
It's the same.

Swordfishtrombone

Words & Music by Tom Waits

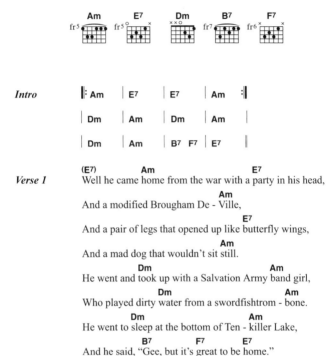

Intro
‖: Am | E⁷ | E⁷ | Am :‖

| Dm | Am | Dm | Am |

| Dm | Am | B⁷ F⁷ | E⁷ ‖

Verse 1

(E⁷)   Am   E⁷
Well he came home from the war with a party in his head,

                     Am
And a modified Brougham De - Ville,

                            E⁷
And a pair of legs that opened up like butterfly wings,

                  Am
And a mad dog that wouldn't sit still.

            Dm   Am
He went and took up with a Salvation Army band girl,

            Dm   Am
Who played dirty water from a swordfishtrom - bone.

            Dm   Am
He went to sleep at the bottom of Ten - killer Lake,

            B⁷   F⁷   E⁷
And he said, "Gee, but it's great to be home."

Verse 2

(E7)   **Am**   **E7**
Well he came home from the war with a party in his head,

                           Am
And an idea for a fireworks dis - play.

                                   E7
And he knew that he'd be ready with a stainless steel machete,

                           Am
And a half a pint of Ballentine's each day.

    Dm   **Am**
Then he holed up in a room above a hardware store,

    Dm   **Am**
Crying nothing there but Hollywood tears.

    Dm   **Am**
And he put a spell on some poor little Crutchfield girl,

    B7   **F7**   **E7**
And stayed like that for twenty-seven years.

Verse 3

(E7)   **Am**
He packed up all his expectations,

       E7
He lit out for California,

                          Am
With a flyswatter banjo on his knee.

With Lucky Tiger in his angel hair,

       E7
And benzedrine for getting there,

                   Am
They found him in a eucalyptus tree.

    Dm
Lieutenant got him a canary bird,

  Am
And skanked her head with every word,

    Dm   **Am**
And Chesterfielded moonbeams in a song.

     Dm   **Am**
He got twenty years for loving her from some Oklahoma governor,

    B7   **F7**   **E7**
Said everything this doughboy does is wrong.

Verse 4

   (E7)   **Am**   **E7**
Now some say he's doing the obituary mam - bo,

                                Am
Now some say that he's hanging on the wall.

Perhaps this yarn is the only thing,

  E7
That holds this man together,

                    Am
Some say that he was never here at all.

Dm   **Am**
Some say they saw him down in Bir - mingham,

Dm   **Am**
Sleeping in a boxcar going by.

   Dm   **Am**
And if you think that you can tell a bigger tale,

  B7   **F7**   **E7**
I swear to God you'd have to tell a lie.

Outro

𝄆: **Am** | **E7** | **E7** | **Am** :𝄇

| **Dm** | **Am** | **Dm** | **Am** ‖ *To fade*

192

Tom Traubert's Blues (Four Sheets To The Wind In Copenhagen)

Words & Music by Tom Waits

F · Gm11 · F/A · B♭ · G7 · C7 · Gm7

Intro

| F | Gm11 | F/A | B♭ | B♭ | |
| F/A | F/A | G7 | G7 | C7 | C7 |

Verse 1

B♭   F/A
Wasted and wounded, it ain't what the moon did,
  Gm7   C7   F Gm7 F/A
I've got what I paid for now.
B♭   F/A
See you tomorrow, hey Frank, can I borrow,
  G7   C7
A couple of bucks from you,
      F   Gm11 F/A   B♭
To go waltzing Ma - tilda, waltzing Ma - tilda,
F/A   Gm11   C7
You'll go waltzing Ma - tilda with me.

Verse 2

        B♭   F/A
I'm an innocent victim of a blinded alley,
       Gm7   C7   F   Gm7 F/A
And I'm tired of all these soldiers here.
B♭   F/A
No one speaks English and everything's broken,
    G7   C7
And my Stacys are soaking wet.
      F   Gm11 F   B♭
To go waltzing Ma - tilda, waltzing Ma - tilda,
F/A   Gm11   C7
You'll go waltzing Ma - tilda with me.

B♭   **F/A**
Now the dogs are barking and the taxi cab's parking,
    Gm7   **C7**   **F**   **Gm7 F/A**
A lot they can do for me.
  B♭   **F/A**
I begged you to stab me, you tore my shirt open,
        G7   **C7**
And I'm down on my knees to - night.
      B♭   **F/A**
Old Bushmill's I staggered, you'd bury the dagger,
        G7   **C7**
In your silhouette window light.
        F   **Gm11 F/A**   **B♭**
To go waltzing Ma - tilda, waltzing Ma - tilda,
F/A   **Gm11**   **C7**
You'll go waltzing Ma - tilda with me.

          B♭   **F/A**
Now I lost my Saint Christopher,   now that I've kissed her,
          Gm7   **C7**   **F**   **Gm7 F/A**
And the one-armed bandit knows.
          B♭   **F/A**
And the maverick Chinamen, and the cold-blooded signs,
          Gm11   **C7**
And the girls down by the strip-tease shows go...
F   **Gm11 F/A**   **B♭**
Waltzing Ma - tilda, waltzing Ma - tilda,
F/A   **Gm11**   **C7**
You'll go waltzing Ma - tilda with me.

          B♭   **F/A**
No, I don't want your sympathy,   the fugitives say,
          Gm7   **C7**   **F**   **Gm7 F/A**
That the streets aren't for dreaming now.
          B♭
And manslaughter dragnets,
            F/A
And the ghosts that sell memories,
              Gm11   **C7**
They want a piece of the action anyhow.
        F   **Gm11 F/A**   **B♭**
Go waltzing Ma - tilda, waltzing Ma - tilda,
F/A   **Gm11**   **C7**
You'll go waltzing Ma - tilda with me.

Verse 6

        B♭   **F/A**
And you can ask any sailor, and the keys from the jailor,

      Gm7   **C7**   **F**   **Gm7 F/A**
And the old men in wheelchairs know.

       B♭   **F/A**
And Ma - tilda's the defendant, she killed about a hundred,

      Gm11   **C7**
And she follows wherever you may go.

F   **Gm11 F/A**   **B♭**
Waltzing Ma - tilda, waltzing Ma - tilda,

F/A   **Gm11**   **C7**
You'll go waltzing Ma - tilda with me.

Verse 7

       B♭   **F/A**
And it's a battered old suitcase to a hotel someplace,

      Gm7   **C7**   **F**   **Gm7 F/A**
And a wound that will never heal.

B♭   **F/A**
No prima donna, the perfume is on,

      Gm11   **C7**   **F**
An old shirt that is stained with blood and whiskey.

      B♭
And good - night to the street sweepers,

     F/A
The night watchmen flame keepers,

      Gm11   **C7** **(F)**
And good - night Ma - tilda too.

Outro

| **F** | **Gm7 F/A** | **B♭** | **B♭** | |
| **F/A** | **F/A** | **Gm11** | **C7** | **F** |

Table Top Joe

Words & Music by Tom Waits & Kathleen Brennan

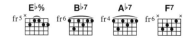

I knew one day,

One, one, two, one, two, three.

Intro

E♭%
Diddly da dee dee,

Da dee dee dee bolay bo day a lay bee.

B♭7
Whoa, yeah.

E♭%
Boddle an day buddle ay dando wa lay.

Verse 1

E♭%
Well, my mama didn't want me on the day I was born,

B♭7   E♭%
I was born without a body, I got nothing but scorn.

But I always loved music, all I had was my hands,

B♭7   E♭%
I dreamed I'd be famous and I'd work at The Sands.

Chorus 1

E♭%
Singing, Tabletop Joe, Tabletop Joe,

B♭7   E♭%
Now every - one will know that I'm Table - top Joe.

Verse 2

E♭%
I had trouble with the pedals but I had a strong left hand,

B♭7　　　　　　　　　　　　E♭%
And I could play Stravinsky on a baby grand.

I said, "I'm gonna join the circus, 'cause that's where I belong",

B♭7　　　　　　　　　　　　E♭%
So I went to Coney Island, I was singing this song.

Chorus 2

E♭%
Tabletop Joe, Tabletop Joe,

B♭7　　　　　　　　　　　E♭%
Now everyone knows, yeah, I'm Table - top Joe.

Bridge 1

　　　　　A♭7　　　　　　　　　　　　E♭%
They gave me top billing in the Dreamland Show,

　　　　F7　　　　　　　　B♭7
I had my own orchestra starring Tabletop Joe.

　　　　　　　　　　E♭%
And the man without a body proved everyone wrong,

　　　B♭7　　　　　　　　E♭%
I was rich and I　　was famous, I was where I belonged, yeah.

Chorus 3

E♭%
Tabletop Joe, Tabletop Joe,

B♭7　　　　　　　　E♭%
Now everyone knows, yeah, Table - top Joe.

Take it home boys.

Ad lib. scat singing

Outro

‖: E♭% | E♭% | E♭% | E♭% |

| B♭7 | B♭7 | E♭% | E♭% :‖　*Repeat to fade*

Take It With Me

Words & Music by Tom Waits & Kathleen Brennan

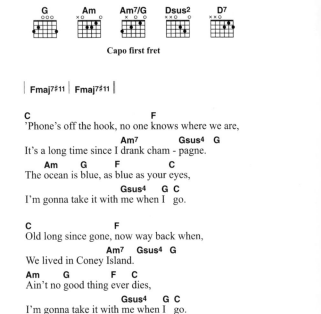

Capo first fret

Intro | Fmaj7♯11 | Fmaj7♯11 ‖

Verse 1

   C   F
'Phone's off the hook, no one knows where we are,
                        Am7   Gsus4 G
It's a long time since I drank cham - pagne.
     Am   G   F   C
The ocean is blue, as blue as your eyes,
                    Gsus4   G C
I'm gonna take it with me when I go.

Verse 2

   C   F
Old long since gone, now way back when,
                     Am7   Gsus4 G
We lived in Coney Island.
Am   G   F   C
Ain't no good thing ever dies,
                    Gsus4   G C
I'm gonna take it with me when I go.

Bridge 1

   Am   Am7/G F   C
Far, far a - way   a train whistle blows,
                 Am Am7/G F   Dsus2   D7   Gsus4 G
Wherever you're going,   where - ever you've been.
                 Am Am7/G F   C
Waving good - bye   at the end of the day,
                   Am Am7/G   Dsus2   D7 Gsus4 G
You're up and you're over   and you're far a - way.

Verse 3

```
C                      F
Always for you, and forever yours,
              Am7 Gsus4  G
It felt just like the old  days.
         Am    G      F      C
We fell a - sleep on Beaula's porch,
              Gsus4    G C
I'm gonna take it with me when I  go.
```

Verse 4

```
C                         F
All broken down by the side of the road,
              Am7       Gsus4  G
I was never more a - live or a - lone.
         Am     G     F      C
I've worn the faces off all the cards,
              Gsus4    G C
I'm gonna take it with me when I  go.
```

Bridge 2

```
              Am    Am7/G F            C
The children are playing      at the end of the day,
              Am    Am7/G Dsus2 D7  Gsus4  G
Strangers are singing      on our  lawn.
              Am   Am7/G F          C
It's got to be more        than flesh and bone,
              Am    Am7/G Dsus2 D7   Gsus4  G
All that you've loved      is all you own.
```

Verse 5

```
C
In a land there's a town,
         F
And in that town there's a house,
              Am7      Gsus4  G
And in that house there's a woman.
         Am   G          F      C
And in that woman there's a heart I love,
              Gsus4    G C
I'm gonna take it with me when I  go.
              Gsus4    G C
I'm gonna take it with me when I  go.
```

Outro

```
| Fmaj7#11 | Fmaj7#11 | C  ‖
```

Temptation

Words & Music by Tom Waits

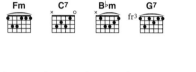

Fm   C7   B♭m   G7

Intro | Fm | C7 | C7 | Fm |

Verse 1

Fm   C7
Rusted brandy in a diamond glass,

      Fm
Every - thing is made from dreams.

C7
Time is made from honey slow and sweet,

     Fm
Only the fools know what it means.

B♭m   Fm C7   Fm B♭m   Fm G7   C7
  Temp - tation,   temp - tation,   temp - tation, I can't re - sist.

Verse 2

      Fm   C7
I just know that she is made of smoke,

          Fm
But I've lost my way.

       C7
She knows that I am broke,

         Fm
But I must play, yeah.

B♭m   Fm C7   Fm   B♭m   Fm G7   C7
  Temp - tation, temptation,   yeah,   temp - tation, I can't re - sist.

Interlude 1   ‖: Fm | C7 | C7 | Fm   :‖

Fm B♭m   Fm C7   Fm   B♭m   Fm
Oh,   tempta - tion, temp - tation, tempta - tion,

G7   C7
Well, I just can't re - sist.

Verse 3

Fm   C7
Dutch pink and Italian blue,

          Fm
She is there waiting for you.

      C7
My will has disappeared,

        Fm
My confusion is oh so clear.

B♭m   Fm   C7   Fm   B♭m   Fm   G7   C7
Temp - tation,   temp - tation,   temp - tation,   I can't re - sist.

Interlude 2   ‖: Fm | C7 | C7 | Fm   :‖

B♭m   Fm   C7   Fm   B♭m   Fm   G7   C7
Temp - tation,   temp - tation,   temp - tation,   I can't re - sist.

Verse 4

Fm   C7
Rusted brandy in a diamond glass,

          Fm
Everything is made from dreams.

        C7
Time is made from honey slow and sweet,

         Fm
Only the fools know what it means.

B♭m   Fm   C7   Fm   B♭m   Fm
Temp - tation,   temp - tation,   temp - tation,

B♭m   Fm   C7   Fm   B♭m   Fm
Temp - tation,   temp - tation,   temp - tation.   *To fade*

That Feel

Words & Music by Tom Waits & Keith Richards

A   D/F#   Esus4   E/G#   B7

Intro | A | A | D/F# | Esus4 ||

Verse 1
A
There's one thing you can't lose,

D/F#   **Esus4**
It's that feel.

    A
Your pants, your shirt, your shoes,

   D/F#   **Esus4**
But not that feel.

D/F#
   You can throw it out in the rain,

      E/G#
You can   whip it like a dog,

A   **D/F#**
   You can chop it down like an old   dead tree.

You can always see it,

      E/G#
When you're coming into town,

     A
Once you hang it on the wall,

    B7
You can never take it down.

Verse 2
      A
But there's one thing you can't lose,

     D/F#   **Esus4**
And it's that feel.

     A
You can pawn your watch and chain,

    D/F#   **Esus4**
But not that feel.

D/F#
  It always comes and finds you,

cont.

E/G♯   A
It will always hear you cry.

A   D/F♯
I cross my wooden leg,

And I swear on my glass eye,

               E/G♯
It will never leave you high and dry,

      A
Never leave you loose,

           B7
It's harder to get rid of than tat - toos.

       A
Verse 3   And there's one thing you can't lose,

    D/F♯   Esus4
Is that feel.

A
   And there's one thing you can't lose,

    D/F♯   Esus4
Is that feel.

D/F♯
You can throw it off a bridge,

E/G♯
   You can lose it in the fire,

A
You can leave it at the altar,

     D/F♯
It will make you out a liar.

You can fall down in the street,

     E/G♯
You can   leave it in the lurch,

    A
Well you say that it's gospel,

   B7
But I know that it's only church.

      A
Outro   But there's one thing you can't lose,

    D/F♯   Esus4
And it's that feel,

   A
It's that feel.

     A
‖: There's one thing you can't lose,

    D/F♯   Esus4
And it's that feel.   :‖   *Repeat to fade*

This One's From The Heart

Words & Music by Tom Waits

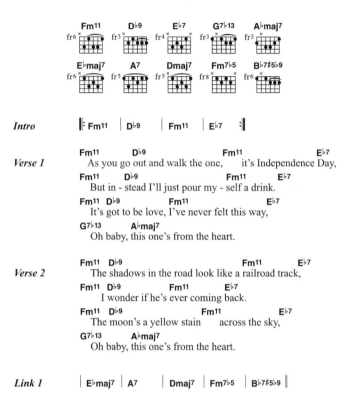

Intro

‖: Fm11 | D♭9 | Fm11 | E♭7 :‖

Verse 1

Fm11   D♭9   Fm11   E♭7
   As you go out and walk the one,   it's Independence Day,

Fm11   D♭9   Fm11   E♭7
   But in - stead I'll just pour my - self a drink.

Fm11 D♭9   Fm11   E♭7
   It's got to be love, I've never felt this way,

G7♭13   A♭maj7
   Oh baby, this one's from the heart.

Verse 2

Fm11 D♭9   Fm11   E♭7
   The shadows in the road look like a railroad track,

Fm11 D♭9   Fm11   E♭7
   I wonder if he's ever coming back.

Fm11 D♭9   Fm11   E♭7
   The moon's a yellow stain   across the sky,

G7♭13   A♭maj7
   Oh baby, this one's from the heart.

Link 1

| E♭maj7 | A7 | Dmaj7 | Fm7♭5 | B♭7#5♭9 ‖

Verse 3

Fm11   D♭9   Fm11   E♭7
Maybe I'll go down to the corner and   get a racing form,
Fm11   D♭9   Fm11   E♭7
But I should probably wait here by the phone.
Fm11   D♭9   Fm11   E♭7
And the brakes need ad - justment on the con - vertible,
G7♭13   A♭maj7
Oh baby, this one's from the heart.

Verse 4

Fm11   D♭9   Fm11   E♭7
The worm is climbing the avo - cado tree,
Fm11   D♭9   Fm11   E♭7
Rubbing its back against the wall.
Fm11 D♭9   Fm11   E♭7
I pour myself   a double sympathy,
G7♭13   A♭maj7
Oh baby, this one's from the heart.

Link 2 | E♭maj7 | A7 | Dmaj7 | Fm7♭5 | B♭7♯5♭9 ‖

Verse 5

Fm11   D♭9   Fm11   E♭7
And blondes, brunettes and redheads put their hammer down,
Fm11 D♭9   Fm11   E♭7
To   pound a cold chisel through my heart,
Fm11   D♭9   Fm11   E♭7
But they were nothing but a - postrophes.
G7♭13   A♭maj7
Oh baby, this one's from the heart.

Verse 6

Fm11   D♭9   Fm11   E♭7
I can't tell,   is that a siren or a saxo - phone?
Fm11   D♭9   Fm11   E♭7
But the roads get so slippery   when it rains.
Fm11 D♭9   Fm11   E♭7
I love you more than all these words can ever say,
G7♭13   A♭maj7
Oh baby, this one's from the heart.

Link 3 | E♭maj7 | A7 | Dmaj7 | Fm7♭5 | B♭7♯5♭9 ‖

Outro   ‖: Fm11 | D♭9 | Fm11 | E♭7   :‖ *Repeat to fade*

Time

Words & Music by Tom Waits

G/B   A7sus4   D   Em7   D/F♯   G

Intro　　　| G/B　A7sus4 ‖

Verse 1
           D
Well the smart money's on Harlow and the moon is in the street,
      G/B   A7sus4   D
And the shadow boys are breaking all the laws.
         G/B   A7sus4
And you're east of East Saint Louis,
          D
And the wind is making speeches,
        G/B   A7sus4
And the rain sounds like a round of ap - plause.
        D
And Na - poleon is weeping in a carnival saloon,
       G/B   A7sus4   D
His in - visible fi - ancee's in the mirror.
       G/B   A7sus4   D
And the band is going home, it's raining hammers, it's raining nails,
       G/B   A7sus4
And it's true there's nothing left for him   down here.

Chorus 1
           D A7sus4 D   G/B Em7 A7sus4
And it's time, time,   time, and it's time, time, time.
           D   D/F♯ G   Em7
And it's time, time, time that you love,
           D   A7sus4 D
And it's time, time,   time.

Verse 2

D
And they all pretend they're orphans and their memory's like a train,

G/B   **A7sus4**   **D**
You can see it getting smaller as it pulls a - way.

G/B   **A7sus4**   **D**
And the things you can't re - member tell the things you can't forget,

G/B   **A7sus4**
That history puts a saint in every dream.

D
Well she said she'd stick around until the bandages came off,

G/B   **A7sus4**   **D**
But these mama's boys just don't know when to quit.

G/B   **A7sus4**
And Ma - thilda asks the sailors,

D
"Are those dreams or are those prayers?"

G/B   **A7sus4**
So close your eyes, son, and this won't hurt a bit.

Chorus 2   As Chorus 1

Verse 3

D
Well things are pretty lousy for a calendar girl,

G/B   **A7sus4**   **D**
The boys   just dive right off the cars and splash into the street.

G/B   **A7sus4**   **D**
And when they're on a roll she pulls a razor from her boot,

G/B   **A7sus4**
And a thousand pigeons fall around her feet.

D
So put a candle in the window and a kiss upon his lips,

G/B   **A7sus4**   **D**
As the dish outside the window fills with rain.

G/B   **A7sus4**   **D**
Just like a stranger with the weeds in your heart,

G/B   **A7sus4**
And pay the fiddler off till I come back again.

Chorus 3   As Chorus 1

Chorus 4   As Chorus 1

Town With No Cheer

Words & Music by Tom Waits

Cm   Cm/B   Cm/B♭   A♭maj7   Cm/G

G7   Fm   Fm/E   Fm/E♭   G7sus4

Verse 1

              Cm   Cm/B   Cm/B♭   A♭maj7
Well it's hotter than blazes   and all the long faces,

          Cm   Cm/B   Cm/B♭   A♭maj7
There'll be no oa - sis for a dry local grazier.

Cm   Cm/B   Cm/B♭   A♭maj7
   There'll be no refreshment for a thirsty jackaroo,

     Cm   Cm/B♭   A♭maj7   Cm/G   G7
From Melbourne to Adelaide on the overlander.

          Cm   Cm/B   Cm/B♭   A♭maj7
With newfangled buffet cars and faster locomo - tives,

        Cm   Cm/B♭   A♭maj7   Cm/G   G7
The train stopped in Serviceton less and less often.

            Cm   Cm/B   Cm/B♭   A♭maj7
No there's nothing sad - der than a town with no cheer.

Cm   Cm/B   Cm/B♭
Vic Rail de - cided the can - teen,

            A♭maj7   Cm/G   G7
Was no longer necessary there,

      Cm   Cm/B   Cm/B♭   A♭maj7
No spirits, no bilge - water and eighty dry locals.

        Cm   Cm/B♭   A♭maj7   Cm/G   G7
And the high noon sun   beats a hundred and four,

            Cm
There's a hummingbird trapped,

    Cm/B♭   A♭maj7   Cm/G   G7
In a closed down shoe store.

Verse 2

    Cm   **Cm/B**
This tiny Victorian rhubarb,

Cm/B   **A♭maj7**
  Kept the watering hole open,

    Cm   **Cm/B** **Cm/B♭** **A♭maj7** **Cm/G** **G7**
For sixty-five years.

         Cm   **Cm/B♭**   **A♭maj7** **G7**
Now it's boiling in a miserable March twenty first,

Cm   **Cm/B**   **A♭maj7**   **G7**
  Wrapped the hills in a blanket of Patterson's curse.

     Cm   **Cm/B**
The train smokes down the xylophone,

       Cm/B♭   **A♭maj7**
There'll be no stopping here.

       Cm   **Cm/B**   **A♭maj7** **Cm/G** **G7**
All you can be is thirsty in a town with no cheer.

Interlude   ‖: **Cm** | **Cm/B♭** | **A♭maj7** | **Cm/G** | **G7**   :‖

Verse 3

    Cm   **Cm/B♭**
No Bourbon, no Branch - water,

         A♭maj7
Though the townspeople here,

Cm/G   **Cm**   **Cm/B♭**   **A♭maj7** **Cm/G** **G7**
  Fought a Vic Rail de - cree tooth and nail.

       Cm   **Cm/B♭**   **A♭maj7** **G7**
Now it's boiling in a mi - serable March twenty - first,

          Cm   **Cm/B♭**   **A♭maj7**   **Cm/G** **G7**
Wrapped the hills in a blanket of Patter - son's curse.

Cm   **Cm/B♭**
  The train smokes down the xylophone,

A♭maj7   **Cm/G** **G7**
There'll be no stopping here.

       Cm   **Cm/B♭**   **A♭maj7**   **Cm/G** **G7**
All you can be is thirsty   in a town with no cheer.

Outro | **Fm** | **Fm/E** | **Fm/E♭** | **G7sus4** |

         | **Cm** | **Cm/B♭** | **G7sus4** | **G7** | **Cm**   ‖

Trampled Rose

Words & Music by Tom Waits & Kathleen Brennan

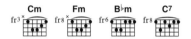

Intro

Cm
Ah, ah, oh.

Ah, ah, oh.

Verse 1

Fm
Long way going to get my medicine,
                                    Cm
Sky's the autumn grey of a lonely wren.
Fm
    Piano from a window played,
                          Cm
Gone tomorrow, gone yester - day.

Chorus 1

B♭m   Fm   B♭m   Fm
I found it in the street, at first I did not see,
B♭m   C7   Fm
Lying at my feet a trampled rose.

Interlude 1

Cm
Ah, ah, ah.

Ah, ah, ah.

Verse 2

Fm
Passing the hat in church,
                      Cm
It never stops going 'round.
Fm
    You never pay just once
              Cm
To get the job done.

	B♭m Fm B♭m Fm
Chorus 2	What I done to me, I done to you,

                   B♭m   **C7**   **Fm**
So what happened to the trampled rose?

                   Cm
Interlude 2   Ah, ah, ah.

                         Ah, ah, ah.

                         Ah, ah, ah.

                         Ah, ah, ah.

                   Fm
Verse 3   In the muddy street,

                              Cm
With the fireworks and leaves.
                   Fm
           A blind man with a cup I asked,

                              Cm
If he'd sing "Kisses Sweeter Than Wine?"

                 B♭m   **Fm B♭m**   **Fm**
Chorus 3   I know this rose like I know my name,

                 B♭m   **Fm B♭m**   **Fm**
          The one I gave my love,   it was the same.

                   B♭m   **C7**   **Fm**
Now I find it in the street, a trampled rose.

                   Cm
Outro   Ah, ah, ah.

                         Ah, ah, ah.

Virginia Avenue

Words & Music by Tom Waits

Fm   B♭7   B♭m   E♭7   A♭7   C7

Intro   ‖: Fm B♭7 | Fm B♭7 | Fm B♭7 | Fm B♭7 :‖

Verse 1

(B♭7)   Fm   B♭7   Fm   B♭7
Well, I'm walking on down Virginia Ave - nue,

Fm   B♭7   Fm   B♭7
   Trying to find some - body to tell my troubles to.

B♭m   E♭7   B♭m   E♭7
   Harold's club is closing, and everybody's going on home,

A♭7   C7
What's a poor boy to do?

Verse 2

(C7)   Fm   B♭7   Fm   B♭7
I'll just get on back into my short, make it back to the fort,

Fm   B♭7   Fm   B♭7
   Sleep off all the crazy lizards inside of my brain.

B♭m   E♭7   B♭m   E♭7
   There's got to be some place that's better than this,

        A♭7   C7
This life I'm leading's driving me in - sane.

            (Fm)
And let me tell you I'm dreaming.

Guitar solo | Fm B♭7 | Fm B♭7 | Fm B♭7 | Fm B♭7 |

            | B♭m E♭7 | B♭m E♭7 | A♭ | C7 ‖

Verse 3

(C7)   Fm   B♭7
Let me tell you that I'm dreaming to the twilight,
Fm   B♭7
   This town has got me down.
Fm   B♭7   Fm   B♭7
   I've seen all the highlights, I've been walking all a - round.
B♭m   E♭7   B♭m   E♭7
   I won't make a fuss, I'll take a Greyhound bus,
A♭7   C7
Carry me away from here, tell me, what have I got to lose?

Verse 4

(C7)   Fm   B♭7   Fm B♭7
'Cause I'm walking on down Columbus Ave - nue,
Fm   B♭7   Fm   B♭7
   The bars are all closing, 'cause it's quarter to two.
B♭m   E♭7   B♭m   E♭7
   Every town I go to is like a lock without a key,
  A♭7   C7
The blues I leave behind keep catching up on me.
                                 Fm   B♭7
Let me tell you they're catching up on me,
                        Fm B♭7   Fm B♭7
They're catching up on me,   catching up on me,
                    Fm B♭7   Fm
Catching up on me,   catching up on me.

Warm Beer And Cold Women

Words & Music by Tom Waits

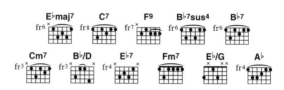

             E♭maj7 C7   F9 B♭7sus4

Intro   One of those nights,

         B♭7sus4   E♭maj7   C7

Verse 1   And it's warm beer   and cold women,

         F9

        No I just don't fit in.

                B♭7sus4   B♭7

'Cause every joint I stumbled into to - night,

  E♭maj7   B♭7 Cm7

     That's just how it's been.

  B♭/D   E♭maj7   C7   F9

All these double knit strangers   with gin and vermouth,

            B♭7sus4   E♭maj7   E♭7 Fm7

And the recycled stories in the Naugahyde booths.

  E♭/G   A♭   B♭7

And the platinum blondes,

               E♭maj7   C7

And to - bacco bru - nettes,

             F9

I'll just be drinking to forget you,

           B♭7sus4   E♭7 Fm7

And I'll light an - other cigarette.

  E♭/G   A♭   B♭7   E♭maj7   C7

And the band's playing something   by Tammy Wy - nette,

         F9   B♭7   E♭maj7 B♭7 Cm7 B♭/D

And the drinks are on me to - night.

Verse 2

E♭maj⁷ · · · · · · · · · · C⁷
All · · my conversations now,

· · · · · · F9
I'll just be talking about you baby.

· · · B♭7 · · · · · · · · · · · · · E♭maj⁷ · · · · · · B♭7 Cm⁷
And boring some sailor as I try to get through.

B♭/D · E♭maj⁷ · · · · · · · · · · C⁷
I just · want him to listen now,

· · · · · · · · · F9
I said that's all you have to do.

· · · · · · · · B♭7
He said I'm better off without you,

· · · · · · E♭maj⁷ · · · · · · · · · E♭7 Fm⁷ B♭/D
Till I showed him my tattoo.

· · · · · A♭ · · · · · · · · · B♭7
And now the moon's rising,

E♭maj⁷ · · · · · · · · C⁷
· · It ain't no time to lose.

· · · · · · · · · · F9
It's time to get down to drinking,

· · · · · · · · B♭7 · · · · · · · · · · · E♭7 Fm⁷
Tell the band to play the blues.

E♭/G · · A♭ · · · · · · · · · B♭7
And the drinks are on me,

· · · · · · E♭maj⁷ · · · · · · · · C⁷
And I buy a couple of rounds.

· · · · · · F9 · · · · · · B♭7 · · · · · (E♭maj⁷)
At the last ditch at - tempt sa - loon.

Sax. solo	E♭maj⁷	C⁷	F9	F9
	B♭7	B♭7	E♭maj⁷	B♭7 Cm⁷ B♭/D
	E♭maj⁷	C⁷	F9	F9
	B♭7	B♭7	E♭maj⁷	B♭7 Cm⁷ E♭/G
	A♭	B♭7	E♭maj⁷	C⁷
	F9	F9	B♭7	E♭7 Fm⁷ E♭/G
	A♭	B♭7	E♭maj⁷	C⁷
	F9	B♭7	E♭maj⁷	B♭7 Cm⁷ B♭/D

Verse 3

(B♭/D) E♭maj7   C7   F9
Warm beer and cold women,   I just don't fit in,

B♭7
Every joint I stumbled into tonight,

E♭maj7   B♭7 Cm7
   That's just how it's been.

B♭/D   E♭maj7   C7   F9
All these double knit strangers   with gin and vermouth,

B♭7   E♭maj7   E♭7 Fm7
   And receding hairlines in the Naugahyde booths.

E♭/G   A♭   B♭7
And the platinum blondes,

E♭maj7   C7
   And tobacco bru - nettes,

        F9
I'll just be drinking to forget you baby,

          B♭7sus4   E♭7 Fm7
I'll light a menthol cigarette.

E/G   A♭   B♭7   E♭maj7   C7
And the band's playing something   by Johnnie Barn - ett,

      F9   B♭7   E♭maj7 C7 F9 B♭7 E♭7
At the last ditch at - tempt sa - loon.

Way Down In The Hole

Words & Music by Tom Waits

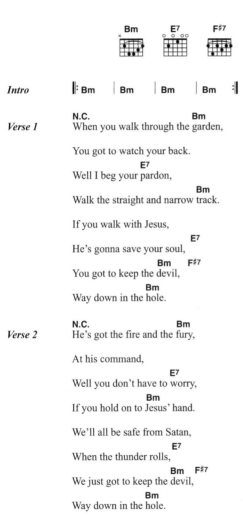

Intro ‖: Bm | Bm | Bm | Bm :‖

Verse 1

N.C.   Bm
When you walk through the garden,

You got to watch your back.

                E7
Well I beg your pardon,

                                        Bm
Walk the straight and narrow track.

If you walk with Jesus,

                                E7
He's gonna save your soul,

                Bm   F♯7
You got to keep the devil,

                Bm
Way down in the hole.

Verse 2

N.C.   Bm
He's got the fire and the fury,

At his command,

                        E7
Well you don't have to worry,

        Bm
If you hold on to Jesus' hand.

We'll all be safe from Satan,

                E7
When the thunder rolls,

                Bm   F♯7
We just got to keep the devil,

                Bm
Way down in the hole.

Guitar solo | Bm | Bm | Bm | Bm |

| E7 | E7 | Bm | Bm |

| Bm | Bm | Bm | E7 |

| Bm | F#7 | Bm | Bm ‖

Verse 3

N.C.   **Bm**
All the angels sing,

About Jesus' mighty sword.
                  E7
And they'll shield you with their wings,
                 Bm
And keep you close to the Lord.

Don't pay heed to temptation,
                E7
For His hands are so cold,
                  Bm   **F#7**
You got to help me keep the devil,
           Bm
Way down in the hole.

Chorus

N.C.   **Bm**
Down in the hole.
        E7
Down in the hole, yeah.
        Bm
Down in the hole, yeah.
        E7
Down in the hole.

Down in the hole.

Down in the hole.
                  Bm   **F#7**
You got to help me keep the devil,
        Bm
Down in the hole.

Guitar solo		Bm		Bm		Bm		Bm	
		E7		E7		Bm		Bm	
		Bm		Bm		Bm		E7	
		Bm		F#7		Bm		Bm	‖

Bm

Outro   Ooh. Ooh.   *To fade*

Yesterday Is Here

Words & Music by Tom Waits & Kathleen Brennan

Am   E   C/G   D9   F   F7   D   B7

Intro

| Am E | Am E | Am E | Am E |

| Am C/G | E | Am C/G | D9 |

| F E | Am E |

Verse 1

(E)   Am   E
If you want money in your pocket,

        Am   E
And a top hat on your head,

    Am   C/G
A hot meal on your table,

            E
And a blanket on your bed.

            Am   C/G
Well to - day is grey skies,

        D9
To - morrow is tears,

            F   E   Am   E
You'll have to wait till yesterday is here.

Verse 2

(E)   Am   E
Well I'm going to New York City,

        Am   E
And I'm leaving on a train,

    Am   C/G
And if you want to stay behind,

            E
And wait till I come back again.

          Am   **C/G**
Well to - day is grey skies,

      D9
To - morrow is tears,

      F   **E**   **Am**
You'll have to wait till yesterday is here.

Bridge

Am   **F7**
If you want to go,

Am   **F7**
Where the rainbows end,

       Am   **E**   **Am**
You'll have to say good - bye.

                 F7
All our dreams come true,

       Am   **F7**
Baby up ahead,

         Am   **D**   **B7** **E**
And it's out where your memories lie.

Verse 3

(E)   **Am**   **E**
Well the road is out be - fore me,

          Am   **E**
And the moon is shining bright.

        Am   **C/G**
What I want you to re - member,

      D   **E**
As I disappear to - night.

        Am   **C/G**
Well to - day is grey skies,

      D9
To - morrow is tears,

      F   **E**   **Am**
You'll have to wait till yesterday is here.

          C/G
Well today is grey skies,

      D9
To - morrow is tears,

      F   **E**   **Am**
You'll have to wait till yesterday is here.

               E   **Am**
You'll have to wait till yesterday is here.

               E   **Am**
You'll have to wait till yesterday is here.

Who Are You

Words & Music by Tom Waits & Kathleen Brennan

D   G/B   Bm   F#m7   G   Asus4

Capo first fret

⑥ = D   ③ = G
⑤ = A   ② = B
④ = D   ① = E

Intro | D | D | D | D   ‖

Verse 1

D
Well, they're lining up,
             G/B   D
To mad-dog your tilt-a-whirl.

Three shots for a dollar, win a real live doll.
            Bm   F#m7
All the lies that you tell,
            G   Asus4
I be - lieved them so well.
            D
Take them back,
                 G/B   D
Take them back to your red house,

For that fearful leap into the dark.
            Bm   F#m7
Oh well I did my time,
            G   Asus4
In the jail of your arms,
            G/B
Now O - phelia wants to know,
            Asus4
Where she should turn.

Verse 2

(Asus4)   D
Tell me what did you do,

              G/B   D
What did you do the last time?

Why don't you do that,

                                G/B   D
Well, go on ahead and take this the wrong way.

Time's not your friend.

        Bm   F#m7
Do you cry, do you pray,

        G   Asus4
Do you wish them away?

        Bm   F#m7
Are you still leaving nothing,

      G   Asus4
But bones in the way?

        Bm   F#m7
Did you bury the carni - val,

        G
With the lions and all?

Verse 2

Asus4   D
Excuse me while I sharpen my nails.

                               G/B   D
And just who are you, who are you this time?

You look rather tired,

Are you pretending to love?

                G/B   D
Well, I hear that it pays   well.

        Bm   F#m7
How do your pistol and your Bible

        G   Asus4
And your sleeping pills go?

        Bm   F#m7
Are you still jumping out of windows,

        G   Asus4
In ex - pensive clothes?

        Bm   F#m7   G   Asus4
Well, I fell in love   with your sailor's   mouth,

        G/B   Asus4
And your wounded eyes.

cont.

        Bm   **F♯m7**
You better get down on the floor,

         G   **Asus4**
Don't you know this is war.

      G/B   **Asus4**   **D**
Tell me who are you this time?

      G/B   **Asus4**   **D**
Tell me who are you this time?

Outro   ‖: **D** | **D** | **D** | **D**   :‖ **D**   ‖